WHITE BITING DOG

JUDITH THOMPSON

PLAYWRIGHTS CANADA PRESS
Toronto

White Biting Dog © Copyright 1984 Judith Thompson

Playwrights Canada Press is the publishing imprint of
the Playwrights Union of Canada (PUC): 54 Wolseley St., 2nd fl.
Toronto, Ontario CANADA M5T 1A5
Tel. (416) 947-0201 Fax. (416) 947-0159

Playwrights Canada Press operates with the generous assistance of
The Canada Council - Writing and Publishing Section, and Theatre Section,
and the Ontario Arts Council.

Front cover photo and design by E.J. Powers
Photo of Judith Thompson by Paul Till. Editors: Ann Jansen, Tony Hamill.
Canadian Cataloguing in Publication Data
Thompson, Judith, 1954 -
        White biting dog
A play
ISBN 0-88754-369-3
I. Title.
PS8589.H4883W55 1984   C812'.54   C84-012939-4
PR9199.3.T562W55 1984

First edition: May 1984
First revised edition: September 1985
Third printing: September 1988
Fourth printing: September 1989
Fifth printing: August 1991
Sixth printing: February 1994
Printed and bound in Winnipeg, Manitoba, Canada.

This play is dedicated to my cousin Katy

WHITE BITING DOG was first produced at Tarragon
Theatre, Toronto, in January, 1984, with the
following cast:

CAPE . . . . Hardee T. Lineham

GLIDDEN . . . . Larry Reynolds

PONY . . . . Clare Coulter

LOMIA . . . . Jackie Burroughs

PASCAL . . . . Stephen Ouimette

Directed by Bill Glassco
Set designed by Sue LePage
Costumes designed by John Pennoyer
Lighting designed by Harry Frehner

WHITE BITING DOG was winner of the 1984 Governor-
General's Award for Drama

N.B. Because of the extreme and deliberate musicality of this play, any attempts to go against the textual rhythms, such as the breaking up of an unbroken sentence, or the taking of a pause where none is written in are DISASTROUS. The effect is like being in a small plane and suddenly turning off the ignition. It all falls down. This play must SPIN, not just turn around.

The Characters:

CAPE   A very handsome silky young man who
            could seduce almost anybody in twenty
            minutes. He is compulsively seductive,
            extremely charming and manipulative.
            He thinks and speaks very quickly,
            changing mental gears constantly and
            with great alacrity. He seems to be
            flirting with everyone he talks to. He
            even flirts with the audience while
            telling them the most terrible things
            about himself. Mid to late twenties.

GLIDDEN   The kind of man others refer to as
            "lightweight." He is kind, loves to
            play pranks and wants desperately for
            his life to be like a Norman Rockwell
            painting. He is dying of a disease
            contracted from the constant handling
            of sphagnum moss -- gardening was one of
            his chief pleasures. In the last few
            years he has realized that people
            constantly patronize him and he fights
            this. Without his wife he has no reason
            to live. Late fifties or early sixties.

PONY   Her clothing should express her
            directness: natural fabrics, simple
            walking shoes, subdued colours, no prints,
            nice lines. Clothes are for comfort, but
            are always neat. Her hair should be out
            of her face, but should not bring
            attention to itself. She is deeply
            ethical. Anywhere from twenty to
            thirty-five or so.

LOMIA   She is not knowingly campy and is not a
           performer. She is obsessed with her
           physical being. She is often very shy
           and girlish as well as nasty and
           powerful. She is buffeted by sensation.
           Her words are out before the thought is
           clear in her head. Her clothes should
           not conform to the stereotype of a
           flamboyant woman. Forty-five to fifty-
           five.

PASCAL   He was brilliant at physics and at chess.
           He strives to approach the world and
           every thought freshly. He spends all
           his time thinking about experience. His
           costume and hair should reflect this.
           He can be of any colour or ethnicity.
           Twenty to thirty.

Author's Notes:

The wall to GLIDDEN's room must be transparent.
Three hard baseballs are on the set.

At the end of Act One, GLIDDEN had intended to
play a prank to amuse his wife. However, because
of his illness, he snaps and goes into his
Australian fantasy for a moment.

On page 3, GLIDDEN makes a sound like a cockaburro
as follows:

                (do)   oo oo oo oo
                (re)   ah ah ah ah
                (me)   ee ee ee ee

He repeats these sounds two and a half times, at an
accelerating noise level.

PONY's song on page 10 is sung to the following tune:

fa   fa   soooo   fa   me/re   fa
You're my   dog   my   dog/gie   dog

fa   me   re   fa   me   re/do   re
I ·   love   ya   sooo   I   al/ways   will

                    re/do   re
              I   al/ways   will

The underlined words in the song are three times as long as the other words.

WHITE BITING DOG

WHITE BITING DOG

Act One

It is dark on stage. CAPE
is drumming on his bongo
drums. He reaches a peak,
stops, doubting the reason
for drumming, starts again,
then stops. Unsure, as if
he had heard a peculiar
noise, he steps a few steps
towards the audience, hands
and body shy, but with a lot
of energy. His voice is
soft and polite, hesitant,
but with a confidence
underneath the gentlemanly
softness.

CAPE: Did it even happen? Sure it happened.
          It happened, I'm not crazy, I know! I
          arrived at the Bloor Street bridge, and
          I climbed up on the wall, right? And

(cont'd)

CAPE: I was gonna do it, I was just about
to jump when I heard this drum sound,
as if the whole city knew, boom boom
<u>boom</u> boom BOOM BOOM BOOM BOOM BOOM BOOM...
(speaks in small strange voice) "I'm
not gonna hurt you." (turns quickly)
Who's that? A cop? There's nobody!
Just! A white dog! Beside me! How
did <u>it</u>...

      "YOU'RE JUMPING TO HELL" the dog,
      the <u>dog spoke</u>.

So I...answered--

      "BUT I'M LIVING IN HELL...ANYWAY."

      "YOU'RE LIVING IN HELL, 'CAUSE YOU
      AIN'T DONE YOUR MISSION."

      "WHAT'S THAT?"

      "TO SAVE YOUR FATHER FROM DEATH.
      TO SAVE YOUR FATHER FROM DEATH."

The dog...spoke! I'm not kidding!
This dog actually spoke she saved
me from the plunge; it was the
weirdest--

        (GLIDDEN rushes out of bed, and
        out of his room onto the
        landing)

GLIDDEN: OUT OF THE TUNNEL, OUT OF THE TUNNEL, OUT OF THE... (makes a sound like a cockaburro; sits down, instructing) We don't pull pussy by the tail, Gliddy, we don't pull pussy by the...

CAPE: Dad? What are you doing?

GLIDDEN: To turn my stomach.

CAPE: What?

GLIDDEN: To turny my stomach, to... (half awakens) Ahhh. What...what...what time is it?

CAPE: It's late, you were sleepwalking.

GLIDDEN: Isn't it way past your bedtime? You have...hockey practice tomorrow at six, don't you? You -- hop it to bed right--

CAPE: DAD WAKE UP. I'm twenty-six years old and the only time I play hockey is Sunday nights with a bunch of dentists.

GLIDDEN: Oh. Yes, of course, I knew that, I was just...having you on! Pulling your leg.

(CAPE fakes a laugh)

Never too old or too sick for a bit of a joke! ...Hey, how about a piece of toast?

CAPE: Toast? No thank you, but I could get you one, if--

GLIDDEN: Me? Oh not for me thanks. I'm for a bit of...booze. (gets drink)

CAPE: Were you having the nightmare? About
            the...boat in the ice?

GLIDDEN: What? Oh yes, no. I -- don't know --
            one dream I had, very nice, was your
            mother, your mother in a taf-taffeta
            dress, green, at a...party... My Gawd
            what a hostess, never let anyone feel
            -- left out, you know? Even the ugliest
            person in the corner, why she'd talk to
            fellas with boils so bad you'd want to
            throw up just looking at them.

CAPE: Why don't I take you to bed?

GLIDDEN: Don't patronize me.

CAPE: I'm sorry. I'm sorry.

                    (GLIDDEN is gripped by pain)

CAPE: Should I get your medication?

                    (CAPE starts to get a drink.
                    GLIDDEN walks across the room)

GLIDDEN: Nope, no, you know -- I think I'm going
            to die tonight.

                    (CAPE turns suddenly)

CAPE: But you can't. You can't you have to
            fight it Dad you have to kick and punch
            and...

                    (CAPE is holding GLIDDEN, shaking
                    him. Peat-moss falls out of
                    GLIDDEN'S pajama top)

            Dad I just don't think that's very funny
            any more.

GLIDDEN: Sorry... It's...cool...on the...
           stomach... It's...

CAPE: (cleaning up) ...I just don't think you
           should do it any more.

GLIDDEN: I'm not...any more, I'm not any more that
           man who designed ships' engines...made
           ya wear your hockey helmet, I'm...I'mmm...
           a rotting tree turning into a swamp, a...

                    (GLIDDEN sways, almost falls.
                    CAPE catches him)

CAPE: Dad!

                    (CAPE pulls his father onto the
                    couch. GLIDDEN lies on CAPE's
                    lap; CAPE strokes his father's
                    forehead)

           There. Just lie for a minute.

                    (Sound of skateboard is heard)

GLIDDEN: What-- What the heck is that sound do
           you know I've heard it every day now
           for...

CAPE: That's a skateboard. Down the steep hill.

GLIDDEN: Ohh. You know I think I should have
           accepted that offer. You remember from
           Australia? Back in-- I think a hot
           country might have understood me. Hey,
           did you know that in Sydney, there are
           nine beaches within the city limits?
           WITHIN THE CITY LIMITS! Nine beaches!

CAPE: Nine!

GLIDDEN: Within the city limits! Yes... Yes
            I even -- have this sort of daydream...
            that...well...I think they might have
            made me Prime Minister of that country.
            Cornball eh?

CAPE: No! No -- I've often thought of running
            for Alderman.

GLIDDEN: ...Sometimes I can even imagine being
            carried on the backs of the miners. I'd
            be Labour, of course, the miners from,
            say...Wogga Wogga -- BUT anyway, it's
            too late now...

CAPE: Not yet.

GLIDDEN: (getting up) Maybe not -- tonight.
            Maybe not tomorrow. But soon. When it's
            you, you know, you know-- You know...
            (pausing at stairs) Are you sure you
            won't have that piece of toast?

CAPE: Yes.

GLIDDEN: Have it your way...ah...don't forget to
            turn out the lights and lock the door
            before you go to bed, eh?

CAPE: (shaking) Dad? Should I...uh...sit sit
            with you? What should I...?

GLIDDEN: Listen. Auntie Grace, remember? When
            Gracey was dying and I wouldn't eat
            wouldn't sleep wouldn't move from under
            her bed, just lay there breathing dust
            she said to me "Glid," she said, "Look
            at the kettle, and think of me. I'm
            WATER now, I will be STEAM." That
            helped. (says it faster, like a kid's

GLIDDEN: (cont'd)
rhyme) Look at the kettle and think of
me, I'm water now, I will be steam. I'm
water now, I will be steam. That's all
it is. (goes into room, returns for a
moment)

CAPE: ...If I save HIM, I save myself,
get it? I don't know why I have been
given this...chance. Me, a lousy
young...lawyer with a wife a wife who --
in the whole of four years of marriage
I did not smile at her once. Not once!
I had never smiled at anyone, really,
except a baby once, on the street. I
couldn't. I -- didn't have the...stuff
to make a smile...rise up. It wasn't
THERE. NOTHING WAS. Nothing was ever
there -- for other people, do you KNOW
what that...I could fake it, of course,
it was simple to make the faces, smiles,
laughter, lust -- I laughed so much, in
fact, that I was...noted for my laugh.
(laughs a very infectious laugh) But
it's tiring, I couldn't keep it up, so at
night in my home, I would sit in the dark,
just sit in the dark on the living room
brown shag carpet and Janis, would sit in
the kitchen, under the light...brushing
her hair. Just brushing and brushing and
brushing... Every day I felt...sicker...
to hear another client -- swallow his
coffee -- to smell the personal, unique
smell of someone's bare head as they
stood next to me on the subway -- was
excruciating pain. That's...the only way
I can express it. I could not be happy.
So, on a Sunday in January, I went into
the kitchen -- she hid her brush, I

CAPE: (cont'd)
said "I think I'll get some popcorn,
hon." She said "That would be neat"
and made a (purses lips as if to say
"mmm") face with her lips that she
always made and I went. I went to the
Don Valley Parkway bridge and was stopped
by a dog. Who gave me a mission: to
save myself by saving my father from
death. So I staged a breakdown, crying
in court, urinating in the waste paper
basket. The firm gave me leave,
Janis has filed for divorce, so here I
am now, and... It's failing. He is...
dying...fast so I'm drumming, I'm
drumming and drumming in the hopes that
the dog -- a dog would hear drums, don't
you think? I KNOW she exists, I--

(GLIDDEN drags a large bag of
peat moss onto the landing, and
starts holding his hands far
above his head and dropping
the moss on himself)

D-duh-Father? Da-Daddy what are you--
(to audience) No, no it's nothing, eh?
He he just...it's -- a...mineral in the
dirt, or...

(GLIDDEN is breathing strangely)

Ohhhhhhh! Oh no, oh no, (grabs GLIDDEN)
Father, Father look at me, listen I,
please! Please don't give in, please--

GLIDDEN: (stands up violently) POP POP POP POP
ROCK ME TO GRAVENHURST ROCK ME TO
GRAVENHURST ROCK ME TO GRAVENHURST ROCK

(cont'd)

GLIDDEN: ME TO GRAVENHURST (opens eyes wide)
I'M NOT A ROCK CONCERT NOT A ROCKABYE
ROCK, NOT A ROCKABYE, ROCKABYE CONCERT,
ROCK ME TO GRAVENHURST, ROCK ME TO...

> (GLIDDEN passes out. CAPE
> catches him and puts him over
> his shoulder)

CAPE: Gravenhurst is where the family's all
buried this is it! It's all over there
is no way out.

> (CAPE dumps GLIDDEN on his bed,
> comes out, returns to throw bag
> of peat moss into his father's
> room, comes out again)

Hear that? Hear that? That's the...
grinding of teeth again -- I -- I bet
it's the devils that my great aunt told
us about, under the Don Valley Parkway,
that's THEIR way of laughing, GRINDING
their teeth -- they're laughing
because they think that they have me but
they don't -- they don't, do they?
'Cause the white dog is coming, she's
coming now oh somebody tell her tell
her I'm in trouble, tell her to
HEEEEEEEEEEEELLLLLLLLLLLP!! -- the drums.
Maybe she'll hear the drums (starts
drumming) white dog, dog from the bridge
oh QUEEN of dogs oh please oh help oh
help oh (stops) It's not working.
What'll I do what'll I -- A SONG! A song,
yes, they sing in CHURCH (sings, to the
melody of Agnus Dei) A -- ahhhhhhhhh
laaaaaaa whiiiiitee dog pleeeeeeeeeease...

> (PONY is heard singing, off.
> She enters, continuing to sing
> until she notices CAPE when he
> says "Hello." CAPE speaks after
> he has heard the word "dog" for
> the second time)

PONY: Your <u>eyes</u> do shine so <u>bright</u> and clear
my <u>dear</u> my Queenie dear 'cause you're my
<u>dog</u> my doggie dog I love ya <u>sooo</u> I
always will 'cause your <u>eyes</u> do shine
so <u>bright</u> and clear my <u>dear</u> my Queenie
dear and I <u>hope</u> you never <u>shed</u> a single
<u>tear</u> my Queenie <u>dear</u> 'cause you're my
<u>dog</u> my doggie--

CAPE: Oh my God! Oh my God that's it this is
IT she's HERE-- (runs out of house)
It's -- it's -- a GIRL!! I guess an
<u>angel</u>, kind of a... Hello!

PONY: Oh!

CAPE: I...heard you sing!

PONY: Oh...

CAPE: Don't be...embarrassed it was...what --
what--

> (Intending to ask PONY what the
> answer is, CAPE suddenly
> realizes that maybe she is <u>only</u>
> a girl)

What -- are -- you -- doing out after --
curfew?

PONY: Curfew? There's no curfew here!

CAPE: Yeah but that guy that guy that strangled
the cheerleader, he's still loose!

PONY: I'm not afraid of some weasel. Who are you?

CAPE: I'M...you <u>know</u>?!

PONY: No.

CAPE: I'm <u>the guy</u>. That lives...here. Who are you?

PONY: Just a girl.

CAPE: <u>Just</u> a girl?

PONY: I think so.

CAPE: I -- don't -- think so, I think -- I mean -- if you're just a girl what are you doing wandering the streets singing songs to a dog?

PONY: Well, to tell you the truth, I'll be honest with ya, I was lying on my fold-out in my furnished bachelor on Albany and I got this UNRESISTIBLE urge to get up and go out for a walk. And when urges like that come along, I listen to them so I did. I just walked where my feet took me.

CAPE: --and they took you HERE?

PONY: Well. I don't feel like walking any further.

CAPE: So you don't KNOW where you're going? (realizes she is an unknowing agent of the dog)

PONY: Not particularly.

CAPE: You're so brave!

PONY: Ha. You obviously don't know me very
             well.

CAPE: What, what do you mean?

PONY: I mean that when you've done one-fifty
             down Thunder Bay Road and ya've jumped
             out and picked up an S.I.D. and watched
             him die right in front of your nose
             going out for a midnight stroll is
             tiddlywinks. Seen?

CAPE: S.I.D.--

PONY: It stands for sudden infant death, and
             it is a very tragic thing.

CAPE.   Oh. You -- you were an ambulance man?

PONY: Only for four years.

CAPE: Only.

PONY: You want to watch me. I'm sarcastic.

CAPE: You saved lives then, you -- you saw the
             m-m-- (uses face and body to indicate
             the word "movement")

PONY: You better believe it. Heck my first
             day on we get a call from this Chinese
             family downtown, eh, so we walk into the
             house and this kid takes us to the
             bathroom and ya know what we see? This
             old Chinese guy sittin' on the toity
             bleedin' from every hole in his body;
             nose ears dink mouth, everything, just
             pourin' out blood, so my supervisor looks
             at me and she goes "That's cute."

CAPE: Didn't all the blood make you queasy?

PONY: Who me? You kidding, dissection was my favourite subject!

CAPE: Yes? Why's that?

PONY: I don't know. It always made me feel -- I don't know, like I was a top model or something.

CAPE: You-- (tries to keep her there) --name! Name, what is your name?

PONY: Daid, Pony. (hits herself) I mean, Pony Daid.

CAPE: I'm Cape, Cape Race. Does -- does that sound -- familiar to you?

PONY: Sure. I even been there. Are you from there?

CAPE: Where? Oh! Cape Race? No. No!

PONY: Well how come you're named for it?

CAPE: 'Cause 'cause you know why? 'Cause I am the way the word sounds, I think. Do you -- think?

PONY: I can see that.

CAPE: You're the first person who could! Hey! Why did you leave the ambulance business?

PONY: I'm not at liberty to say.

CAPE: Oh please?

PONY: Swear you won't reveal it?

CAPE: Swear.

PONY: Speeding.

CAPE: They fired you for speeding an
         ambulance?

PONY: They fired me 'cause they knew I was
         gonna quit and their pride was hurt.

CAPE: Why, why were you gonna quit?

PONY: 'Cause it was a bum operation. Like I'm
         an order-oriented person, eh, a neat bar
         my Dad even called me, and this was the
         slackest outfit I ever saw! Something
         you'd think would be the tightest, and it
         was the slackest! Nobody gave a fig!
         So I said to myself "Pony, if you want
         order you're gonna have to be your own
         boss and that's all there is to it."

CAPE: So NOW, you save lives on your own?

PONY: Kinda. I got my own fix-it stand, for
         things though eh, not people, up at the
         mall, out in Mississauga.

CAPE: Ah...would you -- would you like to
         come in?

PONY: What, for a -- tea?

CAPE: Tea? Sure, sure I can make tea.

                    (Pause)

PONY: Um -- just in case you're a bad guy,
        although I don't think you are, I think
        I should tell you that I have been
        trained by this Vietnam vet -- Herb.

CAPE: Hey! Hey you think I'd hurt you? My
        life is in your hands!

PONY: Pardon?

CAPE: Just a -- manner of speech -- ah -- well!
        Here it is!!

PONY: Well. This is quite the -- bare room.

CAPE: Yeah? Oh yeah we -- Pap and me keep
        breaking things -- a couple of oxes.

PONY: Oh I like a clean room -- although I do
        like the occasional knick-knack. Nice
        clock. Hey, ya dropped your mitten.

CAPE: P-please put that back.

PONY: Why?

CAPE: He ah -- Pap wants it there he -- it's
        been there for over a year, do you believe
        it? Ever since the -- ah -- the old duck
        dropped it when she left -- left. He --
        he thinks it'll bring her back or
        something.

PONY: Poor guy. Is he a little--

CAPE: He -- he's dying. In fact, he is going
        to die tonight, if nothing stops him.
        But you -- you know that, don't you?

PONY: Well -- there is a kind of a creepy
          feeling... Also if I do say so you're
          acting a little -- shook up.

CAPE: Yes, yes I'm very shook up.

PONY: I don't blame you, eh, I'd flip out if
          anything happened to my old man.

CAPE: You understand?

PONY: Oh yeah, like I'm wild about my dad,
          just wild. He's very interesting you
          know. He collected mice!

CAPE: Mice! He was a mouser?

PONY: Kinda. He'd spend all Sundays with them,
          building run-wheels and such. Huh. He
          had two hundred and twenty-six at one
          time. Freaked the mum right out.

CAPE: How many now?

PONY: None any more. My dad had to gas them.
          Not meanly, though. He's the
          projectionist for Kirkland Lake, where
          I'm from. Us kids really lucked out,
          eh, got to watch every film fifteen,
          sixteen times.

CAPE: Look, I can't beat around any more I --
          listen -- if you think I'm nuts just
          leave, but -- I have to ask -- are --
          are you here -- to help us?

PONY: What, you and your dad?

CAPE: Yes.

PONY: Well, not that I was personally aware of.
I guess I could be.

CAPE: Okay, I'm gonna spill the whole boodle
-- as I said, if you think I'm insane
-- just walk away. But every word is
pure truth.

PONY: I'll believe you.

CAPE: Okay. See, I was a lawyer, married,
making money, everything was -- in place;
only trouble was, I have a disease, where
I hated -- I hated living so much my
teeth were ground down to baby teeth.
One day it got so bad that I had no
choice; I went to the Danforth Bridge,
climbed up on the wall, and I was just
about to kill myself when I saw a dog,
a white dog, just sitting there. And
then a real miracle happened -- the dog
-- the dog spoke. She told me that I was
JUMPING TO HELL.

PONY: A white dog?

CAPE: Yeah, a small white dog with bu-blue eyes.

PONY: I don't believe it.

CAPE: You've got to!

PONY: No, I mean I believe what you say, but
I'm freaking out because I had a white
dog, like that, she was probably the
being to which I was very closest of all,
Queenie, and I know she had ESP in her,
things happened all the time, and then
just last month she died then I get
this overpowering urge to come here?

CAPE: The -- the dog told me that to <u>save</u> my
          father was <u>my</u> only hope; if he <u>lives</u>,
          I'm cured, now you've come along, and
          <u>you</u> you've <u>saved lives</u>!

PONY: Boy. Boy I knew something important
          would happen to me sooner or later.
          'Cause -- well -- I feel shy to say it,
          but -- well, I -- yeah. I admit it, I
          I'm a psychic.

CAPE: Yes?

PONY: Yeah!! Like this isn't a very good
          example, but up in Kirkland, whenever I
          wanted the traffic light to change, I'd
          just squeeze my bumcheeks together, eh,
          hard as I could, till I almost passed
          out but it worked, it worked every time.

CAPE: Well!

PONY: Oh, I did bigger things too -- I -- well
          I never used it to save a human life,
          but I a couple times I found out HOW to
          save them.

CAPE: You did?

PONY: Yeah. All I would do is, I would
          concentrate on the question "How do I
          save them?" like a trance and then an
          answer comes out. It's worked three
          times. One was Queenie. That's my dog.
          I hooked right into her mind and she told
          me what was wrong! Another was a private
          matter to do with my brother Wade's
          wife, Linda, and one was when Chrissy
          Pilon was missing and I took them right

PONY: (cont'd)
to the house where he -- the guy --
had her. Now they COULD have all been
like a coincidence, but--

CAPE: No, they weren't. They weren't at all.
You -- are -- here...to save our lives!!
You have...

PONY: I knew it!! I knew I'd do something
special more than work in a mall!

CAPE: ...Could you go into your trance now,
he's very bad.

PONY: Um sure, I don't mind but -- this feels
so -- kinda -- normal, you know? I --
like I wonder if we could have something
for the -- underneathness?

CAPE: Oh yes! Sure. (turns out lights; moves
to drums) How's that?

PONY: That is excellent. You keep on doing
that, and I'll just concentrate real--

(They make contact)

Oh yeah, keep up that drumming, that's--

CAPE: His name is Glidden, Glidden Race.

PONY: Glidden -- Race...okayyy -- mm-mm...

(PONY holds her breath, sways.
They both almost go into trance.
The drumming is spectacular.
PONY shudders and says in LOMIA's
voice, or LOMIA says through a
screen)

PONY: Oooooooooooh that's lovely darling could
           you just do the inside of my arm, oh God
           that is delicious I just made a lovely
           thick fanny burp!

                    (CAPE jumps up, turns on the
                    lights)

CAPE: Ahhhhh! What -- what what was that?

PONY: I don't know, I didn't even hear me, but
           whatever you heard, that's what it is.
           It's what the answer is, I know, I feel
           it.

CAPE: But but but that -- that was my -- my
           mother my oh. That was her voice. That
           was my mother's voice. (almost vomiting)

PONY: Jeeps. You obviously don't get on with
           your mum.

CAPE: But her words came out of YOUR mouth,
           didn't they? What does that mean?

PONY: It means her coming back is the only
           thing gonna save your dad.

CAPE: What?

PONY: I know it, I can feel it in my feet. Oh
           yeah, when I get it that way it's always
           right, right as anything.

CAPE: That means I -- I have to convince her
           somehow to come back for good?

PONY: Yes. Yes it does.

CAPE: But -- but I can't. I can't bring her
         here.

PONY: Why not?

CAPE: Because she's corrupt. You know what she
         did to my father? She fucked around on
         him for years, then dumped him. He
         turned to mush, shaking, sweating all the
         time, the snakes at his office were
         thrilled, saying at their cocktail
         parties he was impotent that's why she
         left. He was turned to mush and it's her
         fucking fault it's FUCK HER. You know
         what I'd do if my dream came true? I'd
         like to get on National TV and tell them
         how she made me drink my own nose bleeds
         from fruity jam jars. She did! And she
         <u>farts</u> like no person should, she -- oh
         <u>dear</u>, I -- I am sorry pardon me. I
         guess the trance-- Look, basically, I'd
         rather she not come back here 'cause I'm
         afraid we'd argue, and that I might harm
         her...

PONY: I thought you said if you saved your Dad
         you wouldn't be strange any more.

CAPE: This is different.

PONY: Just -- don't harm her. Get a grip.

                (The doorbell rings)

CAPE: Who -- who the hell could that be?

PONY: Oh pizza fraud likely. I heard you get
         that all the time down here.

                    (CAPE opens the door. LOMIA and
                    PASCAL are standing outside.
                    PASCAL half whispers throughout
                    the scene and keeps his hands
                    about his face)

CAPE: (whispers, shocked) Mu-um.

LOMIA: (in a hoarse voice) Be-before I explain
            this intrusion could could somebody get
            me a glass of water? I've got tortures
            in my throat worse than-- (coughs)
            Please?

PONY: I'll get it!

CAPE: Mum. (voice and hands shaking)
            What-what-what-what...

LOMIA: Not -- yet, darling, give me a moment,
            I -- oh God I feel dizzy this room is
            so -- empty -- and strange...I -- oh uh
            Pascal could you hold me up OH I feel as
            if I'm gonna fall through the floor it's
            awful...is is your father in Sonny?

CAPE: My father?! I-- What -- Mother! It's
            it's four in the morning it's...

LOMIA: Is it? Well yes, I suppose that is
            unorthodox, but the time is not the...

PONY: Clean water's best thing for a strep for
            sure.

LOMIA: Thank you...is not the point. (drinks)
            Oh. You have no idea what it feels like
            to have a condemned house in one's
            throat -- ah -- Sonny, you've met Pascal,

LOMIA: (cont'd)
haven't you? Yes, yes, that time at the liquor store, with the glasses person -- uh--

CAPE: Mum I-I-I told you then my-my name is Cape now--

LOMIA: (not hearing) Oh! Is that so--

PASCAL: How's it keeping, Cape?

CAPE: Yeah, yeah, Pascal, is that -- ah -- scab permanent or is it there all the time? Ha ha just kidding! We -- ummmmm -- we were just -- ah -- going for a stroll.

PASCAL: It's -- it's -- keen out there, sharp and--

PONY: I can see the two of you have the same virus.

LOMIA: No, no Pascal's chosen to whisper, because the English language is the language of death, right foof?

PASCAL: Like box cars -- shuts out, and kinda locks in. It's corrupt to the -- colon-- (mimes colon)

CAPE: Ha! That's a joke, yes? That's funny, that -- what is a colon again? Oh yeah col -- it -- is -- I--

(LOMIA almost faints)

Mum? Are you -- are you all right? Wh-why are you in your nightgown?

LOMIA: We've just been -- in a fire!

CAPE: What?

LOMIA: My ankles are still shaking...look!
           Look!

CAPE: MUM what HAPPENED your your place burned
           down?!

LOMIA: It was blocking our path to the -- ohh.
           It made everything so BRIGHT and...

PASCAL: It was white. White fire. Like being
           tied to a stake. I know how the --
           witches felt--

CAPE: Here Mum, put this under your head, you--

LOMIA: My heart was just -- pounding it was SO
           terrifying, nothing could describe it,
           nothing -- the cat, Blacky died, he
           choked right in front of us and oh GOD I
           mean we think that the girl in Theology
           down the hall with that light red hair
           she -- she had to take pills to sleep so
           she might have-- Oh I hope NOT I mean
           we just ran we-- Oh sorry darling I
           guess I'm talking your head off I -- I
           guess I'm in shock, is this shock? Yes,
           I guess we're both in -- shock. I mean
           shock. Oh.

PASCAL: The cat clawed her throat -- look! Maybe
           trying to get -- in! Her.

LOMIA: Ohhhhh. The worst thing is that it was
           all my fault!!

PONY: (to herself) I'll get some blankets.

                    (CAPE gestures to his old upstairs
                     room)

CAPE: (puts his arms around Lomia) No, no,
          don't say that. I'm sure it WASN'T.

LOMIA: But I ASKED HIM TO LEAVE!! Geoffrey,
          this -- speed freak acquaintance of
          Pascal's.

PASCAL: He was...depressed.

LOMIA: And we felt sorry for him but -- well we
          finally HAD to ask him to leave after
          three weeks, nicely of course, and he did,
          but then, about seven hours later, I
          smelled something, and no, we hadn't left
          the burner on, so I looked at the door
          and -- there were these little black
          curls -- I opened it and this -- monster
          of black smoke hurled itself at me!!
          OH I -- darling could you give me a
          little room?

                    (CAPE has been sitting too
                    close)

CAPE: Oh. So -- sorry. I must -- my body
          odour must--

LOMIA: It's just that I'm extra-sensitive
          after the fire -- and...

CAPE: You and...smells. Once she stayed in the
          Four Seasons for a week because they were
          painting next door...

PONY: (gives blanket to LOMIA) Ma'am...

LOMIA: It wasn't a week.

PONY: Sir? (gives blanket to PASCAL)

LOMIA: Oh thank you so much. (coughs)

PASCAL: The fire escape was burning hot, the
          metal you know, and it didn't even go
          all the way down!! We were choking
          and we had to jump over a storey!

CAPE: But Mum your hip?

LOMIA: It's bad -- I -- that's why I was
          hoping -- well you -- you don't mind
          if -- if we -- sleep on the couch or
          -- the kitchen table or something, do
          you?

PONY: Oh, well ya couldn't go anywhere else
          now, you--

LOMIA: Pasc was wanting to sleep in an old
          Lincoln Continental--

PONY: Biggest car on the road--

CAPE: Ummmmmm. Um um um. (he is upset, but
          covering it)

LOMIA: What's the matter?

CAPE: Just-- (gestures towards her and PASCAL)

LOMIA: Oh. Well, I-I think it'll be okay. Your
        father can handle this sort of thing.
        They may not have met but they have talked
        on the phone, and it IS an emergency,
        and--

CAPE: But -- he's ill right now. The shock of
        having the two of you--

LOMIA: God, he's not THAT flimsy, I mean we're
        still very good friends, and--

CAPE: He's got a bad influ-enza!

LOMIA: But darling, this is an emergency!

PASCAL: (stays cool) Let's go to Dupras, Lom.

LOMIA: No, Pascy, I don't like his dog!

PASCAL: What's wrong with it--

LOMIA: He sprayed his -- what do you call it
        -- white on my leg, at the dinner table.
        Anyway, there is plenty of room here!
        Just, Sonny, if you would just go -- wake
        him up and ASK him, I'm sure he wouldn't
        hear of us leaving. He -- don't look at
        me like that -- heavens -- PLEASE, Sonny,
        if I don't get some sleep right now I
        will catch tuberculosis, you know my
        resistance to germs is extremely low.

CAPE: Would you just -- keep your VOICE down?

LOMIA: Don't talk to me that way GOD I -- my
          mitten! My mitten! I don't believe it!
          Oh GOD this is the mitten I lost last
          year, remember? I must have left it here
          when I dropped off the Christmas gifts
          -- God I missed this mitten so much. I
          went the whole winter with one hand in
          a pocket I-- Isn't it beautiful?

PONY: That's a very nice mitt.

LOMIA: Oh! Darling, you've forgotten to
          introduce us to your friend!

CAPE: No I didn't, I wouldn't do that, I oh.
          Didn't I? Sorry, um -- Pony, this is my
          mother and her slave, Pascal. Just
          kidding.

                    (LOMIA, in her refusal to see
                    unpleasantness, laughs
                    genuinely)

LOMIA: Ha ha, ha HA.

PASCAL: I've seen you on the streetcar.

PONY: How's it going, Pascal? Please to meet
          you, Mrs. -- sorry, I didn't catch the
          last name--

LOMIA: I don't have a surname of my own! No
          woman ever has. I'm Lomia.

PONY: Oh. Boy, that's a handsome name.

LOMIA: Yes, like -- LAMINATE -- or something.
          Hee! You -- are broad-shouldered -- do
          you -- um -- throw -- shotput or swim or
          something?

PONY: That is really strange you should ask
         that 'cause just yesterday I was thinkin'
         I should get back to swimming -- see
         back in Centennial I won five golds--

LOMIA: FIVE GOLDS? You must have very strong
         -- pectorals -- or -- wait a minute,
         are you two -- no, the two of you
         aren't--

CAPE: Mother.

LOMIA: And I was starting to think you left
         Janis because you were -- odd-- Well I
         think that is just marvellous. You have
         my blessings whether you want them or
         not. (kissed them both) Now I'll just
         go and wake up your father -- I think if
         I explain to him, he'll--

                 (CAPE runs in front of his
                  mother, and makes a grotesque
                  face and noise. This must
                  not be clowny or comic)

LOMIA: You haven't done that since you were
         seven years old.

CAPE: Yes I did I just did it now. Ha ha ha!

LOMIA: I -- really didn't expect you to be
         so -- shook up by us -- coming here
         together I -- I'm...

CAPE: I'm not shook up.

LOMIA: All right, then let me past so I can
         wake your father...if you won't let me
         past, I'll have to call him. Okay, here
         I go, GLIIIIIIIIIIDEN, GLIDDDDDDDENNNN,
         GLLLIIIII...

                    (CAPE runs to PONY, takes her
                    hand)

CAPE: I don't think I can make it, I can <u>hear</u>
            them <u>grinding</u>, I don't think I can <u>handle</u>
            her.

PONY: Don't fret, I'm <u>here</u>.

PASCAL: I'm splitting, Lom. I can't -- deal --
            in -- this -- shit!

LOMIA: All right, all right, I give up. I
            surrender. I'll go to sleep like an
            animal in doorways 'cause my very own
            son wants me out of his...GLIDDEN!

                    (GLIDDEN, wearing a large bathing
                    suit, walks down a ramp or
                    stairs in time to music, singing
                    the familiar tune)

GLIDDEN: <u>If...I...knew</u> -- <u>you</u> -- <u>was</u> -- comin' --
            I'd -- a -- BAKED a cake, baked a cake,
            baked a cake! If I knew you was comin'
            I'd a BAKED A CAAAAAAKE-- How'd ya do,
            how'd ya do how'd ya dooooooooooo...

LOMIA: A...bit ragged, actually, darling. Is
            this for the -- amateur musical?

GLIDDEN: (kisses LOMIA on the cheek) Wh-what a
            pleasant surprise darl I-I was lying in
            the sack and I heard your...mellifluous
            voice -- and I said to my-myself...I
            think a little...en-entertainment is in
            order but ah -- I-I guess nobody's
            laugh-laughing, eh, LAUGH! Will-will
            ah anybody have a drink? Piece of toast?

PONY: (pause) I ah...don't eat toast myself, sir.

LOMIA: Gliddy Sonny tells me you're not well, that you're--

GLIDDEN: Nonsense! So, let me take your orders, what'll it be? Darl?

LOMIA: I-I don't think anybody -- oh yes, I'll have one, you know, that much water (indicates lots) that much gin. (indicates a little)

(GLIDDEN turns to PONY)

CAPE: Oh. Dad, this is my friend PONY she -- she went to law school with me.

GLIDDEN: Go-good to meet you -- I-I bet you didn't see much of my son in the law library he-he spent the whole time down with the...pinball machines! Can I get you two barristers a drink?

(PONY shakes her head)

CAPE: Not for me.

LOMIA: (drinks) Thank you, pooch. Glidden you don't look well at-- (feels his forehead) Oh Lord it's a hundred and three at least, poor -- here -- look, (takes coat) wear this--

GLIDDEN: No thanks darl. I'm just fine, I--

LOMIA: No, look, I insist, I--

                    (LOMIA tries to put the coat on
                    GLIDDEN. He runs away, but she
                    slowly pursues him. He trips
                    and almost falls, and she stops)

GLIDDEN: No, no thanks darl.

LOMIA: Please just...okay, if you really don't
           want it, I--

GLIDDEN: Oh. You must be--

PASCAL: Yes. I'm Pascal.

GLIDDEN: Heard you were...slim, yes. Yes...

LOMIA: He's not -- that -- thin.

GLIDDEN: Well he's not exactly fat, is he?

LOMIA: No. No. I -- where are you going?

GLIDDEN: To put-put in the toast, how many pieces
           you--

LOMIA: NO! Please, please Glidden I have to --
           tell you something I -- look, couldn't
           everybody please just -- leave us --
           Glid and I alone for a moment.

                (They all stand still)

PONY: Um. I think the gentleman should take
           this blanket first.

LOMIA: Yes, yes take mine please.

GLIDDEN: All right, all right. Now you heard
what the lady said, go dig a hole to
China-- SCAT. SCAT!

CAPE: Come on Pony.

> (He takes her hand, and they go
> into another room. PASCAL
> pauses, opens the front door,
> goes out. LOMIA and GLIDDEN
> are left alone)

GLIDDEN: Well. I -- I see you found your mitten!

LOMIA: Yes! Yes I was sooo happy I -- really
missed it I -- you'll think I'm mad but
I liked it so much that I just wore the
one the whole winter -- I kept my other
hand in my...pocket...I...thank you!
Thank you for not...throwing it out.

GLIDDEN: Well, I...know how much you...liked those
mittens.

LOMIA: Yes...I -- did. I do....oh Glid. I'm
sorry it's been so long.

GLIDDEN: Ohhh that's all right, I--

LOMIA: And coming at this time, and--

GLIDDEN: Well knowing you I didn't expect you to
come at tea time!

LOMIA: No, no, I...

GLIDDEN: And I'm...glad to have met your...

LOMIA: Good. He...wanted to meet you too...I
            talk about you so much...

            (Pause)

LOMIA: I...really would have visited more often
            but I...just...well, I think of you, and
            it's as if...I'd...seen you. You know?

GLIDDEN: Oh yes. Yes I've...experienced that,
            all right. Yes...

LOMIA: And the phone is still anathema to me
            for some reason I just hate using it...

GLIDDEN: I know about you and phones. I guess
            you got a case of telephonaphobia?!
            (laughs)

LOMIA: Yes.

GLIDDEN: You look like a dream!

LOMIA: Me? No, I'm fat, aren't I?

GLIDDEN: Huh hoo I'm not falling into that trap.
            If I say you're thin, you'll say that
            means you were fat before. If I say you
            look nice, you'll say I mean you look
            plump, because I like a plump...

            (LOMIA starts to cry)

            Why are you crying?

LOMIA: (upset) Be-be-- Oh I didn't want to
bother you with it and -- and -- look I
was going to come visit you soon I
mean -- I mean I certainly never would
have come like this with Pascal but
they -- they torched us, Glid. They --
murdered our home. We were almost burnt.

GLIDDEN: What? Who did that--

LOMIA: A little boy he -- he spread gasoline
round our door when we were sleeping and
then -- and then -- then I woke up and I
smelled something and I didn't know what
it was, then a rat _ran_ across the
floor with his back on fire, screaming,
so, so we ran in our nighties down the
fire escape and watched, we watched it
burn down and -- and --

GLIDDEN: Lomia, are you telling me that your-your
place has been burnt down?

LOMIA: YES!! I -- so we had nowhere to sleep
so -- oh I feel so BADLY about bringing
him here, but I-I don't have any other
friends. You are my only other friend.
My women friends all loathe me for some
reason. They turn their eyes away when
I start to talk. (crying)

GLIDDEN: Now now -- for God's sake stay here as
long as you like. You're welcome both of
you...really you -- you're still sharing
a place with this fellow, then?

LOMIA: Oh yes.

GLIDDEN: Yes? Well, I'm glad you're not alone.
             I know you don't like to be alone.

LOMIA: No.

             (LOMIA strokes her nightgown,
              smiles, looks away)

GLIDDEN: Oh. I'll bet you could do with a loan
             to -- cover your losses, eh?

LOMIA: Oh. If you could afford it we would be
             grateful--

GLIDDEN: Who, moneybags? Of course I can
             af-af-afford it and yes-- (forgets what
             he is saying) I'll ah-yuh, and in the
             meantime you you can bunk down in Cape's
             old room.

LOMIA: Sonny doesn't want me here. He hates me.

GLIDDEN: I think hate is rather a strong word.

LOMIA: It's true. You should have seen him!!
             My own son detests me!

GLIDDEN: Oh no, no. He's just...not over his
             breakdown -- poor kid, still right in
             the thick of it.

LOMIA: Poor...BABY! When I read your letter
             about him coming back home I-- I just
             cried and cried but then I -- thought
             well, maybe he hated law, I mean it
             is pretty dull, and I don't think he
             was ever in love with Janis -- maybe a
             breakdown was the only feasible <u>escape</u>,
             may--

GLIDDEN: You haven't had to live with the
            drumming.

LOMIA: Drumming? (sees drums)

GLIDDEN: Oh yes he's become a...what do you call
            it...a Beatle. Yes...he just drums and
            drums. And-- (notices her sadness)
            Hey there -- don't you worry about him
            hating you because it's just not...look,
            I'll call him in. CAAAAAPE, say CAAA--

LOMIA: When did he start using that name?

                    (CAPE enters)

CAPE: When I got sick of the name you named me
            'cause your mind was a blank.

LOMIA: Ohhh -- sweetie it was just really 'cause
            your squished little face didn't remind
            me of anything so I didn't want to BRAND
            you with--

CAPE: Well I'm Cape now. Okay?

LOMIA: Well I can't call you that.

CAPE: Okay, then. Do you mind if I call you
            Meatloaf?

GLIDDEN: I'm warning you...

LOMIA: It doesn't matter love.

GLIDDEN: Cape tell your mother you are happy to
            have her and her friend stay in your old
            bed for as long as they...

CAPE: Certainly, if they don't mind the mould.

LOMIA: No! No I don't mind mould at all -- I
           -- it's just like all the other gunk in
           the air only bigger, isn't it? I mean
           they say your eyebrows are just CRAWLING
           with--

CAPE: My eyebrows aren't crawling with
           anything.

GLIDDEN: I said tell your mother you are happy.

CAPE: Of course I am. She knows that.

LOMIA: Yes. (kisses him) I do. Know it...
           Well. I'm glad that's settled. Now
           let's get the sickie to bed! (feels
           GLIDDEN's forehead) Oh dear you're just
           burning!

GLIDDEN: Sickie my foot. I'm going to bed because
           it's way past my bedtime. To hell with
           the rest of you. Never was sick a day in
           my life before fifty. Not even a cold.

                    (LOMIA and GLIDDEN exit. PONY
                    enters)

PONY: Is she staying?

CAPE: I guess so.

PONY: Well not much thanks to you!! Jeeps you
           almost wrecked your chances.

CAPE: I know.

PONY: You can't let your feelings get in the
           way of the mission!!

                    (CAPE is trembling)

PONY: Jeepers. What's wrong?

CAPE: It's it's taking ALL my strength not to
          (puts hand up as if to hit) <u>hurt</u> her.

PONY: I think you're exaggerating.

CAPE: Tell me what I should do.

PONY: Just leave. Once you're finished your
          mission, just go! You're too old to be
          living home anyways! It's nothing. I
          know a lot of people whose mothers bug
          'em.

CAPE: (to himself) I never could leave a room
          she was in.

PONY: I think you could do a whole lot more
          than you think you could do. I think--

LOMIA: Fell asleep soon as his head hit the...
          Sonny! You're looking so saad! (plays
          with him) Don't be sad. Tomorrow we get
          to throw out a whole hour. Did you know
          that? The man at the all-night fruit
          store told me? Or is it we ADD a whole
          hour. Anyway. (big clown smile to make
          him laugh) Hee hee hee! So! We're
          gonna take your old room, poop, mould or
          no mould.

CAPE: How many hours are there in the shortest
          day?

LOMIA: I don't know, four or five? Where's
          Pascal? PAAAAAAAAAS CAL!

                    (LOMIA opens the front door
                    and looks for PASCAL. He steps
                    in)

PASCAL: I told you not ever to shout!

LOMIA: Shhhhhhhhh!! Everything is fine,
           they want us to stay.

CAPE: I hope I didn't make you feel unwelcome.

LOMIA: We understand, don't we foof? If we have
           any change in our schedule at all we're
           sick for a week!

PASCAL: Sure -- well -- I wouldn't let us -- in,
           ummmm considering.

CAPE: It's nothing to do with that at all.

           (Pause)

LOMIA: Yes, well I'd love to stay up with you
           kids and chatter, but if I don't get
           this throat to sleep right now it'll pack
           its tonsils and run away!! Just like
           you used to, you crumb-bum!

CAPE: I never ran -- ran away!

LOMIA: You did so! Don't you remember the time
           you were away all day? I had the whole
           fire department out looking for you --
           and you just appeared at about five with
           six pieces of bubble gum in a brown paper
           bag. I don't know where you got them.

CAPE: ...And you cut them up, cut 'em up and
           then we buried 'em in the back 'cause
           you said that they would grow to
           dinosaurs under the ground and then step
           out just in time for my birthday party!!
           Jesus. Jesus.

PONY: Jeeps. Did you really do that Lomia?

LOMIA: Oh yes. Yes! Did you ever run away,
           Pony? (she is stroking herself
           unknowingly)

PONY: Oh I used to be out the door and down the
           street every chance I got! That's what
           my mum tells me.

CAPE: Mu-um?!

LOMIA: Yes.

CAPE: Stop doing that--

LOMIA: What? (realizes what she's doing) Why?

PASCAL: I -- I'm really wasted Lom.

LOMIA: When caveman calls! This way foof,
           you'll drip over this room!! (exiting)
           I'm sooo happy I found my mitten!!

PONY: What a truly beautiful lady!!

CAPE: Is she? All I'm aware of is her
           nose-hairs.

PONY: You are something, you know that? Behind
           her back you say you hate her like poison,
           then I see ya with her and it seems like
           ya really like her!!

CAPE: Well I don't. And it does not really
           seem like it...does it?

PONY: I can see how ya'd feel strong about her
           -- she's got kinda a profound fume about
           her.

CAPE: She's e-stranged.   Just like me.
(pause) We're both -- happiest
kind of -- staring into space! (mimes
exaggerated staring)

PONY: Well, you must just be a couple of
space puppies!!

> (CAPE is totally absorbed in his
> own thoughts)

Hey...I was just being sarcastic really
-- I know what ya mean about staring, I
used to sing whenever my mum was giving
me heck, just sing right in her face,
from the top forty. (sings) "Indiana
wants me, Lord I can't go back there"
and she's yelling...yeah... Yup... Um.
Hmmmm. Oh, ohhh jeeps I'd better be
off--

CAPE: No!!

PONY: But -- but I gotta be out at the plaza
eight o'clock a.m.!

CAPE: No! I -- want, want you to stay. There's
something -- I don't know. Most women
look right through you, unless you treat
them like shit. Not you, not you.

PONY: I -- never noticed that.

CAPE: Mmmm. Your head smells like--

PONY: Dirty hair?

CAPE: ...stale hay, kinda like stale hay, but
good, nice, beautiful, you know? In
fact, you are -- hey, are those acne

CAPE:
(cont'd)
scars? -- just kidding-- Why did I say
that -- I-- Christ, I almost -- feel
something -- moving -- Pony Pony do you
feel it?

PONY:
(breathless) I don't really like to say
these things out loud.

CAPE:
(kisses her) Oh. Oh oh. That was --
almost -- good. That was...

PONY:
(stops) What about your wife Cape?

CAPE:
My wife? She...we're not married
any more. She's okay. She's okay.
Really. (gasps) What if he dies
tonight? (resolves to take action)
After all this is over, we'll go to
Cape Race!

> (PONY smiles. CAPE goes into
> his father's room, looks at
> GLIDDEN sleeping. PONY shyly
> moves to the couch, sits down,
> then falls asleep)

Daddy?

GLIDDEN:
(bolts upright) What's happened what's
happened!

CAPE:
Nothing--

GLIDDEN:
Who who who who who was that on the
phone? (rushes out to landing)

CAPE:
I came up to tell you a secret.

GLIDDEN:
A secret what, are you stoned again?
Been -- in-injecting oranges with my
vodka again and -- and diluting the bottle
with water? I can always taste that, you
know, I--

CAPE: Dad you're time travelling.

GLIDDEN: What?

CAPE: SHHHHHH. She might hear.

GLIDDEN: Who?

CAPE: Mum.

GLIDDEN: Oh. You mean she WAS here, it WASN'T a--

CAPE: (whispering) She's STILL here. She was
            in a fire, remember--

GLIDDEN: Yes. Yes. Uh oh. My...hair wasn't...
            up on the one side, was it?

CAPE: You looked dashing.

GLIDDEN: That's a load of crap.

                    (One beat. CAPE does not reply,
                    but continues)

CAPE: Look I have to tell you...she told me
            just now that she wants to leave that kid
            and come back with you!

GLIDDEN: When...when. When did she...tell you
            this?

CAPE: Just now...she was crying in the bathroom
            and I asked her why and...she told me!

                    (It occurs to GLIDDEN that this
                    could be a function of his son's
                    breakdown)

GLIDDEN: Why -- doesn't she come up and tell me
            this herself?

CAPE: 'Cause she wants to break it up with the
            kid tonight, and then offer herself to
            you at lunch tomorrow! That's what she
            said!

GLIDDEN: No she must be in shock from the fire
            these things are...look, why don't you
            just go to bed.

CAPE: Dad I'm telling you the <u>truth</u>.

GLIDDEN: If you told her about my illness I'll
            knock your bloody head off.

CAPE: No, of course not, although if you want
            to keep it a secret I wouldn't do your
            dirt thing in front of her.

GLIDDEN: Don't be cheeky. Are -- are you sure
            you're telling me the truth?

CAPE: I swear on my life.

GLIDDEN: You do? (beat) Well -- this...certainly
            will change things...

CAPE: Yes...I hope it will.

GLIDDEN: So my wife is coming back to me. I
            can't believe it you know, I can't
            believe it.

CAPE: Tomorrow; <u>sleep well</u>. (exits)

GLIDDEN: Why would she want -- to come back to me?

                    (CAPE comes downstairs, starts
                     drumming and praying to himself.
                     PONY wakes)

PONY: Pardon? What?

CAPE: Hello.

PONY: Hi.

CAPE: You were right.

PONY: He needs her back? I knew it.

CAPE: So what do we do?

PONY: We can't make her do something she
         doesn't want to do!

CAPE: Well we just might have to because if
         we don't, HE <u>DIES</u> (stops drumming) and
         I'm off the <u>BRIDGE</u>. Today. Do you want
         me to jump off the bridge?

PONY: Of course not, but -- well, to tell you
         the truth I don't think ya would. I
         think you'll be able to handle his dying
         a lot better than you think you can.

CAPE: You don't believe me! You don't believe
         how bad my life was!

PONY: A lot of people live in pain, Cape, and
         you don't see <u>them</u> jumpin' off bridges.

CAPE: YOU DON'T KNOW WHAT THIS WAS LIKE:
         SUICIDE WAS IMPERATIVE. (stops drumming)
         If we don't get her back, I will -- be
         -- dead. Do you -- want that?

PONY: No I -- definitely do not.

CAPE: (caresses PONY erotically) Then you're
         going to stick by me?

PONY: (slowly nods, aroused) I guess I will.
Yeah. I will.

CAPE: (caresses PONY) Who said missions were
easy? Eh?

PONY: Nobody.

CAPE: So help me now. Go into your thing--

PONY: Okay. Okay, I'm ready if you're ready.
Ready?

CAPE: Ready.

> (CAPE turns out the lights, holds
> PONY's hand, and drums)

GO! (drums) And -- tell us more to
catch the whore, tell us how to get the
sow, anything at all we'll give to make
my father live oh live oh more the whore
and how the sow and--

> (PONY stands up. She is her
> twelve-year-old self giving a
> speech)

PONY: Umm -- this speech is called the White
Biting Dog on account of that's what my
dog is. That's Queenie so um -- here
goes -- Linda! We all know you like
Randy, you don't have to talk to him--
Excuse me Miss Birdsall -- anyways,
something about that dog. I'm so close
with her I almost am her, although I'm
not as good a barker, ha ha and um I
never bite, just jorshin', I mean -- uh
oh, that was supposed to come later oh
cripe, I did this, Miss, I just oh geep
I have to sit down.

CAPE: (turns on light) What was that?

PONY: Freak-me-right-out!

CAPE: Who who who was it?

PONY: It was me. Grade Seven public speaking,
            only I turkeyed it up on account of I had
            a temperature that day -- hundred and
            three, two before death. Whew. Ever
            weird.

CAPE: But WHAT THE HELL DOES IT MEAN? Mean?

PONY: I don't know, maybe nothing.

CAPE: Nothing? What are you talking about?
            It's gotta mean something, you were sent
            here by the white dog and that was about
            the dog just -- Christ just please tell
            me whatever comes into your head, now,
            anything. ANYTHING!

PONY: Anything?

CAPE: Yes!! (makes hand gesture meaning "come
            on") Yes!

PONY: Well -- I -- don't know, I -- just think
            you should go tell your mum the whole
            thing. Go on her human pity, she'll come
            back.

CAPE: Tell my -- mum?

PONY: That's what I -- feel is right, yes!
            That's what I think.

CAPE: I am not going down on my knees to that
            bitch.

PONY: Did you never see Jason and the Golden Fleece? Come on, you're at least as strong as that guy--

CAPE: (change in attitude) Why are you helping me?

PONY: 'Cause you're a good head.

CAPE: I'm not a good head, I'm a creep. I'm using you to escape, I'M USING YOU.

PONY: No you're not. You need me. That's all.

CAPE: YOU BORE ME. You're from the lower class "eh," "eh" -- you're wearing fake wool and desert boots for fuck sake you're laughable!! Just -- go home to Kirkland Lake. Just go, you hear me? GO HOME. Go home to K-K-kirkk to-- (opens front door)

PONY: --do you really want me to?

CAPE: Yes!! I want to flub this fucking mission it's stu-stupid -- why shouldn't I jump off the bridge, I'm a fucking creep. I don't like anything anyway!

PONY: You like me.

CAPE: I -- do?

PONY: Yes, I think you do. I think you're fine. Do you really want me to go?

CAPE: No!! No I don't-- Oh Christ I'm sorry, I'm sorry Pony I please don't listen to me when I say those things I -- I didn't mean it,

CAPE: (cont'd)
any of it I -- I do do like you, you're
right, I -- you're the only woman, I've
even felt a spark with...

PONY: Look. I only want to stay if--

CAPE: If I put my penis in your sweet sweet
thing and I rub it up and down till it
bursts? AHHHHHHHH! I don't believe I
said that. What a fuck, what a dumb
look, I -- I want you. I'm -- I'm even
sweating, and I don't ever sweat!

PONY: I don't know why you keep whippin'
yourself.

CAPE: Pony. How can I beg her?

PONY: YOU CAN. I know ya can. And don't
worry, ya won't kill her.

CAPE: I won't?

PONY: Nope. You won't. Now go on and ask
her... (steers him)

CAPE: She better say yes. I've told him that
she already did.

PONY: You did?

CAPE: I had to! To keep him-- (holds her
face tenderly) You -- you know if we
-- win -- then I'll be able to -- love
-- you.

          (They touch erotically, and he
          leads her to a bedroom)

CAPE: Would you -- wait for me?

                    (PONY goes into the room. CAPE
                     shuts the door and runs upstairs)

         Mother? Mum? (gags at sound of their
         lovemaking)

LOMIA: What is it?

CAPE: Ah -- sorry to bug you but -- I must
         tell you something.

LOMIA: Tell me in the morning!

CAPE: I have to tell you now!

LOMIA: Just -- go to bed. I'll see you in the--

                    (CAPE throws open the door.
                     LOMIA shrieks)

PASCAL: If you really want it, man, stay and
         watch!

CAPE: I'm sorry but it's imperative that I
         speak to my mother!

LOMIA: Get out this instant.

CAPE: You are coming with me. (pulls her
         roughly) And don't you try and stop me,
         hoodlum.

LOMIA: Let go of me. I'm going back to--

CAPE: You're coming with me whether you like it
         or not, young lady. (places her in chair)
         Now, in future, you come when I call!

LOMIA: (giggles) You are sooo ridiculous, you haven't changed a bit.

CAPE: Don't say that. (shakes her)

PASCAL: Are you -- you -- okay, lamb?

LOMIA: Just -- go to bed, foof.

PASCAL: You sure?

LOMIA: Yes. Go!

PASCAL: You (points to CAPE) You are very -- conservative -- you know that? (bolts back to bedroom)

CAPE: Now pay attention. I have something to discuss with you.

LOMIA: Well it just so happens that I am not up to discussion; not only is my whole body trembling with the need for sleep but my baby teeth are screeching in pain! I will not be subject to your abuse, understand? Good. Night. (starts to exit)

CAPE: You don't take anything seriously, do you? Do you?

LOMIA: Awww. What would you like to tell me, baby, that Miss Opal said your drawing of a horsey was very bery good? Well I couldn't care less, it looks like a blob to me!!

CAPE: I would like to tell you -- that father is dying. (he has her in his control)

LOMIA: --what?

CAPE: They gave him a week to live three
        months ago. He should be dead now.
        Dead. Now.

LOMIA: What-what-what is he -- dying of?

CAPE: His insides are rotting. It's Latin
        for that. In-something.

LOMIA: He -- is he -- he isn't in much pain,
        is he? Is -- he?

CAPE: What do you think?

LOMIA: Oh. Yes, of course.

CAPE: He told me that he would live if you
        came back. Back to stay.

LOMIA: ...Don't. Don't do that to me.

CAPE: (looks at her) If he doesn't know, who
        does, Mummy? HE WOULD LIVE IF YOU CAME
        BACK. DO YOU WANT HIM TO DIE?

LOMIA: No!! No of course not but -- but it's
        his pain I'm worried about, not his
        death. His DEATH would be a favour --
        he can be what he wants then, a red
        cardinal, or a wrinkle in your sock,
        even a vowel, on the floor of my mouth,
        or -- he'll be all right then, it's
        his PAIN--

CAPE: It's your <u>duty</u> to save his life.

LOMIA: Hah!! Awww when you were little you
           used to sit in the hallway, playing with
           your orange truck, and every time I
           passed you on my way to do something
           you'd say "Hello Mummy!" as if you hadn't
           seen me in months, "Hello, Mummy!!" Hah.
           You are such a <u>good</u> son to be so worried
           about your father -- look. I know it
           would be -- nice -- for him to die
           believing that I loved him the way he
           wanted. It would be very nice, but I
           respect him far too much to lie to him.
           Can you understand that? LOOK. He will
           be loved more than you can imagine when
           he's in after-life, I won't matter a
           bit!! Really! He'll -- he'll never
           have to sleep alone, again, think
           they'll all sleep together inside a --
           peach!! Glid and all the dead mothers.
           Just think, admiring him...and...

CAPE: What creepy bullshit.

LOMIA: No, no it's not--

CAPE: Ha. Where do you reckon you'll go after?
           Satan's crotch?

LOMIA: <u>No</u>, cheeky, I'll go to Purgatory, and
           for me, I know exactly what that will be.
           It will be having to wear itchy itchy
           wool right next to my skin on a hot humid
           day with...

CAPE: Cut the <u>crap</u>. Are you saying that you won't come back?

LOMIA: Darling, I have to take care of me. I am my caretaker, I -- I have nightmares about widows--

CAPE: YOU ARE NO DIFFERENT THAN A <u>SEX</u> KILLER.

LOMIA: What an -- ugly and unfair thing to say! You don't--

CAPE: YOU MIGHT AS WELL RAPE AND STRANGLE A LITTLE CHILD.

LOMIA: NO!! NO NO NO!! (attacking, aggressive) You don't understand I can't!! (crying) I can't come back not to save a <u>thousand</u> lives--

CAPE: WHY?

LOMIA: Because I <u>love</u> him. <u>I love him</u> that is stronger than--

CAPE: WHAT ABOUT DAD? Didn't you love Dad?

LOMIA: Dad -- Glid was -- codeine. Pascal is--

CAPE: What? What?

LOMIA: He -- he spikes my blood. I don't know, it's unsayable.

CAPE: He'll drop you like a hot faggot.

LOMIA: He will NOT, he ADORES me. He lives for my footsteps.

CAPE: You're old. Your arms are like bat's wings.

LOMIA: Sonny, when that boy touches my breasts--

CAPE: You don't feel anything.

LOMIA: What?

CAPE: You've never felt anything! Not on the inside you know that.

LOMIA: I-- what a -- weird weird thing to say. Of course I feel, I feel intensely, I--

CAPE: No you don't. Not for others, and neither do I. We can't help it. Nothing-gets-in.

LOMIA: Yes it does, it does get in, it, certainly does it -- no it doesn't you're right. You're right. (whispers the next line) I hate saying it though because saying it -- sort of makes it true, no? I want to, I try to feel things -- I hate it in here, in this -- thick -- pitch -- everything I do, I do to get OUT. Are you the same?

> (CAPE pulls LOMIA to him and kisses her on the mouth, not sensually but as if he's inhaling her)

We -- we -- touched tongues.

CAPE: (holding her closely, starts in a whisper) I'll tell you one thing I feel. I feel-- I always feel-- I want to take you by the hair (does so) and then and then bash and bash and bash and bash and bash your head against the wall till you--

LOMIA: (backs away) What?--

                    (There is a knock knock knock at
                    the door. CAPE opens it. It is
                    GLIDDEN, drunk, on all fours
                    with a big bone in his mouth.
                    He drops it, and speaks, à la
                    Churchill)

GLIDDEN: Rally up, Australia... There's a great
          work to be done... A nation, to be
          built up...and won...underneath...this
          ...southern...sun... (to LOMIA) Eh?
          How 'bout it, toots? Give a dog a bone,
          eh? Give a dog a bone!! (to audience)
          Ohhh I do like a well-turned ankle!

                    Three beats before blackout.

Act Two

> GLIDDEN, dressed up in a
> tux, has set the table
> beautifully. He is holding
> a fork up in each hand, and
> is very excited.

GLIDDEN: Funny how my...little trick worked. I
first learned to do it when I was seven
years old and my best buddy Tommy fell
out of our tree and next the next day
I was sent to Ashbury where-where my
feet were always cold and I was called
"figface" and had to sleep in wet
sheets and missing Mummy and Grace
so...fiercely -- that's when I first
learned to-to always...expect the worst.
Start-start with little things, see,
expect there to be no hot water, not to
find your socks, then move up to dinner
expect only dog food, expect to have
bloody nightmares then a merely "bad"
dream, is really quite good! Look
forward to nothing, and backward to
nothing and it's all...okay. Like a
nice train ride. So I...yes, I...
expected my wife to leave me, a
beautiful woman like that? I used to
run home at lunch every day just to see
if she was still there. Do you think
I expected that heaven to last? That
heaven of phoning up from work at five
o'clock. And saying "Darl, I'm through!
Shall I pick something up on the way
home?" And her saying "Yes pooch, a
loaf of brown." No no she had to escape

GLIDDEN: (cont'd)
that -- she had to escape being -- bored.
I was -- boring. Of course she left.
I certainly NEVER ever expected her to
come back!! That's the...thing of it,
eh? It's the way things just work, the
fates love to be tricky to give, give you
that which you do not expect. Even now,
I don't...dare to believe that she loves
me, not yet, only that perhaps she...
likes me -- I have made some contribution
to my field, after all and...I'll tell you
a moment in time like this makes me feel
that there really is some spirit of good
about...cornball, eh? The one other time
I have felt this...spirit...is when my
son, my son was young and I watched him
eat. I used to...love...to see him eat.
(jumps back into the here and now) Uh oh!

(GLIDDEN sees his forks, places
them, and rushes back to the
kitchen. PONY and CAPE step
out of the bedroom. They have
made love. They kiss)

CAPE: I've never even liked a woman till I met
you, you know.

PONY: No. How come?

CAPE: I'm -- ashamed of this but -- women to me
were just sort of cysts -- dermoid cysts?
I read about them, they're female
hormones, just hair and oil and teeth,
all in a -- cyst -- hah. That's all
women were to -- me. That's all.

PONY: Jeeps. You musta had a bad experience playin' doctor or somethin'.

CAPE: Or maybe they were that way. Not you though you are so -- good! I want to be like you, you're perfect.

PONY: No I'm not.

CAPE: Yes! Hydra thighs and all! (slaps her bottom) Shit. No, really, you are, you're perfect. Per--

PONY: I have bad qualities.

CAPE: What?

PONY: I don't like Jews. There was this family in Kirkland, the Wibbys? They lived out by the shoe factory, eh? So once me and Sherry got this can of rust proofer from her brother and we painted all over their windows with it. Then we grabbed their eleven year old Darlene? She was already havin' her period and we didn't yet, so we wanted to see what she was like, eh, so we took her to Sherry's parents' master bedroom. Everything was blue velvet, and we made her strip. Then we cut off all her hair because it was so blonde and we stuck it to their windows.

                    (CAPE laughs through his nose. PONY laughs, shyly, in turn. He laughs harder, so does she. He caresses her, and they start necking)

PONY: Oh. Oh. (pulls him down to floor, is
         very passionate, then quickly jumps
         away) Oh no -- Gol...oh no!

CAPE: What's the matter?

PONY: I was right! Like last night -- in...
         the middle...it was so...beautiful...I
         was scared. I was scared 'cause I knew
         I'd do anything...ANYTHING AT ALL...for
         that...feeling again...not just sex.
         It's the thing with you -- didn't matter
         that you're married. It was like we
         were upside down in one of them big
         Nova Scotia waves -- I was scared 'cause
         I thought I'd do...real...bad for that
         feeling...ANYTHING, then I thought
         things'd look different in the morning
         and they did I thought they did but
         then just now when you were rubbing me
         down I got that again, I got that big
         wash and I know. I know now that I
         would. That somethin' has hatched
         and -- I would...do ANYTHING...for...to
         get that feelin' again. That I got with
         you. So...I'm no different than when we
         did that to Darlene, no different at
         all, see?

CAPE: (grabs her wrists tightly) What we did,
         it wasn't bad, Pony. It was beautiful
         like you said. It was ecstacy.

PONY: It's...it's probably a sin to like me
         the way I am now, you know, a sex fiend,
         a home wrecker, it's probably...
         (shaking, teeth chattering)

CAPE: PONY. Get a grip on yourself. Like you
         told me-- Get a--

PONY: You want me to? You want me to? For
you, I will. I will even though knowing
what I know about myself hurts worse
than sharp sticks shoved up under all my
nails, I'm gonna get a grip. Cape.
'Cause I love you. I love you more than
anything else on this earth.

                (GLIDDEN, bringing in a cake,
                 sings Herb Alpert)

GLIDDEN: You say this guy, this guy's in love
with you youuuuu -- this guy's in
looooove...who looks at you the wayyy
I do, tell me now...

CAPE: (gasps loudly) Oh no he thinks that Mum
is gonna -- Dad!! He-he -- good morning!

GLIDDEN: How-how does it look?

CAPE: Ace, ace. Is this for--

GLIDDEN: I thought a-a -- sense of occasion would
be nice.

CAPE: Dad -- remember Pony?

GLIDDEN: Yes, yes. You must be starved! Will
ya -- stay to lunch? (goes to get
another chair)

CAPE: You look so, so well!

GLIDDEN: I feel -- like a young Sequoia -- and
-- your mum always loved me in a tux, so
I thought -- why the heck not. What've
I got to lose? (whispers) She's --
probably breaking it off with that fellow
now -- he'll be okay. Your mother always
was good with human feelings--

(LOMIA and PASCAL open the
bedroom door. The others
hear LOMIA and PASCAL about
to come out. CAPE looks
desperately at PONY)

PONY: Uh-uh -- pardon my nose sir but as a
previous paramedic I don't think you
should eat a thing. I think you should
go to bed.

GLIDDEN: Pardon? Oh no I feel better than I've
felt in twenty years.

(LOMIA enters with PASCAL.
Wearing an old private school
sweater of CAPE's, she stretches)

LOMIA: GOOD morning everybody. Ewww I feel all
cakey. GLID! You're up and about!
What are you...

GLIDDEN: Your presence, milady, has had a
PANACEAN effect.

LOMIA: What a charming thing to say. You look
so elegant...what a WONDERFUL set-up
what's it--

GLIDDEN: In honour-honour of you--

CAPE: Ready baby? Watch me die.

PONY: Use your brain -- make it right.

CAPE: Why? I go down she goes with me.

GLIDDEN: I -- thought what the heck let's go to
town after all these things only happen
once... Good morning, Pascal. Did you
sleep well?

PASCAL: What? Oh -- my -- eyes are kind of --
filmy -- um, scratchy, you know, but
I can...see--

GLIDDEN: I'm glad of that. Did you sleep well?
No, I already said that. I mean are
you -- ah...no hard feelings, eh?

PASCAL: No hard...oh, about the <u>mould</u>? No -- no
I'm hon-honoured to be here and -- and I
just...want to tell you -- that um --
you -- you look just like my old home
form teacher and -- we really -- liked
him... He was a good -- human.

GLIDDEN: Good! That's good, would you like to
stay to lunch? That is if it's not too
painful for you?

PASCAL: Painful? OH! Oh she's told you oh no,
my ulcers -- shrunk now -- I can eat
even...pizza so lunch'll be...

GLIDDEN: La? Wouldn't we like Pascal to stay to
lunch?

                    (LOMIA has been arranging things,
                    looking in the kitchen)

LOMIA: Of course! As long as he promises not to
drool!

GLIDDEN: THAT is a jab at ME, I'm afraid...I
always had my elbows on the table.

LOMIA: Pony! Did you have a deep sleep?

PONY: Well, not very, really.

LOMIA: I'm sorry, you must be...tired...

GLIDDEN: (claps hands, puts on party hat) WELL. As master of cere-mony, I would like you all to...get the heck in your seats!! Last one there's a dirty rotten so and so!

> (CAPE and LOMIA run to the table. CAPE puts on a party hat)

LOMIA: Yes sirreeeee sir!

PASCAL: Oh my stomach is contracting like a snail? When you...touch it...?

PONY: You're not whispering today.

PASCAL: No. No. It wasn't right. I'm re-thinking it.

LOMIA: He's searching, right foof? Gliddie this is CHAMPAGNE!!

GLIDDEN: I trust there are no teetotallers here?

LOMIA: Eeeee. I always feel champagne in my ankles first.

CAPE: So did Janis. My ex-wife.

LOMIO: Janis didn't have ankles, just one long calf! Sorry, that was mean.

PONY: In Hawaii, thick ankles are a sign of great beauty.

GLIDDEN: Well may I be so BOLD as to propose a toast?

LOMIA: Carumba!

GLIDDEN: Lomia!

CAPE: To us!

PONY: Each of us!

PASCAL: Yipyoooooooooo! (trying to show he can have a good time) Yip -- yip (building) yip yip-- Yipyooooo!

CAPE: Pascal you're the life of the party! Well I'm gonna hork back some of that cake. (takes some)

PASCAL: The icing is so white; like the great shark -- um -- almost mean -- um. I mean...in my...personally.

GLIDDEN: Thank you Pascal what a nice head of hair you have. (to others) Guess who made it?

LOMIA: YOU?

GLIDDEN: Mrs. Ainsley!!

LOMIA: She still comes? OH I couldn't be in the same room when she was cleaning, what was her perfume? Fer-mented armpit mixed with SPIC and SPAN?

GLIDDEN: We called her Atom Bomb!!

LOMIA: Oh YES!! And remember her favourite snack was cold chicken fat, right from the pan?! She would--

CAPE: I thought she was cool.

LOMIA: She liked you very much. (pause)

PASCAL: Being-being a cleaning lady must be very...hard on the...skin of your knees, I would think.

GLIDDEN: Yes. (serves himself cake) Well, since speeches would bore us all to sleep, I'm going to share a little joke.

LOMIA: Joke! I don't believe I've ever heard you tell a joke!

GLIDDEN: (cuffs her playfully) Okay, which's it gonna be, wide-mouthed frog, or horses and coal? (pause)

PONY: Ah -- horses and coal sounds good!

GLIDDEN: Then horses and coal it is. Well. There was a horse and his -- no -- that's not it -- there was a -- hold on, hold on a second-- Hang on a moment, I'll have her in a minute-- (paces)

CAPE: Mother you sound like a pig in a slop-trough.

(LOMIA looks up with horror, puts more cake in her mouth, chews it carefully and swallows)

LOMIA: Do I? (pause; leaves table, goes to window)

GLIDDEN: I've got it! Heh! Look at your mother. I bet she's hoping to see a red cardinal!! Heh heh! SO -- there were these two magnificent white palominos, and there they were, both fillies, down in the basement of a beautiful castle counting

GLIDDEN: (cont'd)
an enormous pile of coal. One, two
(blanks; rises) I wonder if you'd excuse
me for a moment--

PONY: (walks over to LOMIA) I -- ah -- nothing
-- ah -- personal but -- ah -- may I
inquire as to how much you might weigh?

LOMIA: Pardon?

PONY: I -- didn't mean that I mean -- jeesh
what's wrong with me I mean -- I want to
know what it is you have when you walk
into a room you -- make me feel as though
I'm flying in my sleep, you know? Do
you -- know what that is? Maybe...

LOMIA: It's because I -- love being inside of
my six layers of skin; it's de-licious
in here -- everytime I breathe I sort
of -- breathe out seeds, seeds. I
feel -- I inside I feel like... (honest)
...like...sewage.

(GLIDDEN re-enters, and
immediately speaks)

GLIDDEN: And a thousand more to go! Well suddenly,
just like that, two eggs went flying
overhead in the sky, and these prize
horses they looked at each other...

LOMIA: (to PONY) It's true.

GLIDDEN: ...and what in the hell do you think they
said? They said, "tsk, tsk, tsk."
(pause)

PASCAL: (clapping) Beautiful!! Soooo --
layered -- and -- um--

CAPE: I've never understood it.

GLIDDEN: Neither have I!

LOMIA: (lighting up) From over here it sounded
wonderful! (kisses him) I'm so happy we're
friends again, pooch. This is really fun.
(kisses his cheek, puts on party hat)

GLIDDEN: (pulls her onto his knee; in funny voice)
Get in your place woman!! That always
gets a rise out of her! Well darl, I
guess we might as well tell them now, eh?

LOMIA: Sure! What?

GLIDDEN: She's playing innocent -- WICKED woman--
(whispers to LOMIA) Don't worry, I'll do
it I -- seeing as my wife is too shy, I
would like to make a little announcement
-- concerning the both of us concerning
our -- Mr. and Mrs.-ness -- we...are...
going to be...living together again...as
man and wife and it has made us both...
very happy. Hey a real Lucille Ball this
one, you know what she told me? She
promised, cross her heart and hope to die,
that she will never take another book of
mine into the bath and get all the pages
wet. Now if you have ever seen my wife
reading in the bath, and I trust that you
haven't, you know that that promise is
well let's just say--

LOMIA: No Glidden. (takes his hand away)

                    (GLIDDEN makes a funny face as
                    if he is about to be hit, then
                    points to LOMIA)

GLIDDEN: She doesn't like to be teased.

LOMIA: NO GLIDDEN.

GLIDDEN: (looks at her in a very "couple" way)
          My-- (points to his hair, to where
          dandruff would fall, and brushes off a
          bit) --no?? posture, oh am I -- uh oh,
          by your faces, I've committed quite the
          stumblebum. I -- oh no. Oh NO oh darn
          I -- this is very embarrassing. Mr.
          Pascal -- will you accept my apologies --
          I just presumed that my wife had -- told
          you I -- I don't know what to say I --
          if there's any way we can make it up to
          you -- I -- please feel free to come to
          our home as often as you-- Hey! What
          are you doing for Christmas next year I--
          Lommy makes a very good hard sauce, it's
          her specialty, isn't that so, Lom, now
          what's in it, brandy, icing sugar--

LOMIA: ...Glidden...

GLIDDEN: Yes.

LOMIA: What -- what gave you the -- idea that I
          was...coming back to you?

                    (Pause. GLIDDEN, in total shock
                    and humiliation, gets up slowly
                    to leave the room. After about
                    three steps, he stops, cocks
                    his head, and shuffles to the
                    window)

GLIDDEN: Goddamn it those dingoes are out best get those sheep in! (goes towards front door)

LOMIA: What's happening?

GLIDDEN: Allllright, darl, you can go after them, but for goodness sake if you see an Abbo on walkabout don't run, they're faster than cheetahs, but give him a dollop of cooking fat and he'll be your friend for life. Oh yes, they're big on fat. They...put it on their heads as... decoration. Fat hats! Heh. They're a happy people as a whole, the coloured people, happy...and content... (pause, a bit woozy) So. I guess the two of you will want to hop off and see what you can sal-salvage from the blaze! Here, let me give you that cheque now in case you need to buy some new "threads" -- ya -- can't go around in our honeymoon nightie forever!! Heh. I -- trust you'll stay until you find another place?

LOMIA: Oh... Well. We -- we would be very -- grateful -- are you -- sure you don't mind?

GLIDDEN: Mind? Why should I mind? If you can't be good friends with your estranged wife who can you be good friends with?

(GLIDDEN exits. CAPE starts to go out to bridge)

LOMIA: Sonny, speaking of -- dingoes, are the kids still in the freezer?

(CAPE stops, decides to try one
other thing to get his mother
back, turns, and puts up his
hand as if taking an oath)

CAPE: This spring, I promise, I will bury them
this spring. (stays at door, facing
into room)

LOMIA: It has been three years!

PONY: Who are the kids?

LOMIA: Our dachshunds! Erica, Gretchen and Hans
-- we had them for twelve years and they
were all three murdered by a man in a
what-do-you-call-it -- topless car. The
poor things were bacchic, gobbling up
each others' viscera, dying all over the
road and all -- oh GOD all that that man
could do was to say "Sorry." Ooooh.

(GLIDDEN returns with a cheque,
and puts it on table)

PASCAL: Dogs scare me.

PONY: Oooh they can probably smell it on you
you know, they smell fear; it's a proven
fact. They also smell softiness and
that's exactly what they smell on me.
I'd do anything for a dog.

GLIDDEN: (in pain) La! Give us a funny from
your Ladies Home Business.

LOMIA: No, Glid, you know I can't tell jokes --
anyway I think it's time we-- (knocks
over glass)

(Still at the door, CAPE is
desperate to rock the boat)

CAPE: Excuse me Mother I wonder if you should
consider while searching for apartments
what your "roommate" has been --
spreading -- behind your back?

PASCAL: (stands up, begins small giggle) You...
you, you people have a very complicated
sense of humour don't you? And I'm
beginning to catch on. Oh yeah, oh yeah,
you're not leaving me behind 'cause I get
it...I get it, see, I--

CAPE: Who's talking humour Pascal? I'm talking
...filth.

LOMIA: Lay off him -- chit!

PASCAL: (to himself) Who's talking humour Pascal
I'm talking...filth. (quieter) Who's
talking humour Pascal I'm-- Oh yeah, filth,
right! I know what you mean, you mean
what I'm telling everybody in town, what
I've been spreading around. Yeah I get
it you mean about her being the the the
the the the WHORE OF BABYLON!! Yeah, yeah,
like my crowd is all been wondering who
it is, eh, and what do you know? It's
the lady that lives with me, me...

GLIDDEN: This is worse than horses and coal.

CAPE: Mum, I suggest you discuss this with
the young man yourself, this is no--

PASCAL: And you guys should have seen the fridge,
it was crammed with these jam jars full
of blood? Got to be the blood of saints

PASCAL:
(cont'd)
right? And who keeps the blood of
saints? -- the WHORE OF BABYLON!! GO
FOR IT!! St. Sebastian, St. Albans, St.
Jude, St. Martin, St. Simeon, St. -- I
mean there's no room for milk, what's a
boy supposed to think?

GLIDDEN: What the hell kind of humour is...

LOMIA: It's the new humour I guess.

CAPE:
Except it's no joke is it Pascal?
Anyway, chief, don't fret, that's not
saint's blood, that's just nosebleeds.
Our fridge use to be full of them too
except we use to drink them.

LOMIA:
Nosebleeds? Beef juice! It's supposed
to be very good for you, it said so in
the...

PASCAL:
So so hey! Is my humour on? Do I get
to join the club -- do I...

CAPE: Mother I know my allegation to be fact.

PASCAL:
WHAT, what? That she's the WHORE OF
BABYLON?

LOMIA:
Well. We will decide whether or not
I'm the Whore of Babylon at dinner.
Right now, if we want to find an
apartment, we have to get started.
(picks up coat) And Cape, beef juice
IS VERY good for you. (leaving) They
did a study.

GLIDDEN:
At least come and have a look at the
tiger lilies.

LOMIA: Tiger lilies? I didn't know you'd grown tiger lilies, pooch, I <u>love</u> tiger lilies, they always make me sort of want to... sit on them, you know? Come on foofy!! It's okay!

PASCAL: See, I can do the humour too...I can...

> (Before exiting, PASCAL turns back and takes a step towards CAPE. He is shaking)

I just...you...how did...do...do...you want me to bring you back something? Choc...chocolate? (takes a deep breath; smiles) I'm perpsiring.

> (PASCAL exits, leaving CAPE staring after him)

PONY: What is going on, Cape?

CAPE: I'm not...sure.

PONY: Why...why am I so ready to lie with ya and trick and cause trouble between two nice couples and humiliate a good man? Why...what's happened in me that I even <u>like</u> doing it?? I get <u>off</u> on it, I... (starts to leave)

CAPE: You DON'T get off on it! (grabs her) Listen. Do you have a worst nightmare? Tell me your worst nightmare!

PONY: Why?

CAPE: Tell me!

PONY: Why?

CAPE: Tell me.

PONY: (eyes closed) Well, I go home, right?
And there's these guys, these tough
guys drinking Lemon-Lime on the porch,
and one of 'em's holding a carp, a
great big brown carp, and I look down
the mouth, and there are my folks!
My parents, movin'...their lips for
help, all squished in a carp fish.
And the guys are laughin'.

CAPE: Yes. Well imagine that nightmare, never
ending. Not when you wake up, not when
you go to the bank, or ride your bike,
the intensity never lets up. How long
could you stand it?

PONY: Not...very long.

CAPE: Well neither can I. So help me end it.
PONY. I want to love you...

PONY: I believe you do, Cape.

CAPE: Okay. There is one move we have left.

PONY: To...ki-kill Pascal?

CAPE: You wouldn't kill Pascal for me, Pony,
and DON'T think you WOULD.

PONY: I--

(LOMIA and PASCAL can be heard,
leaving)

LOMIA: (off) 'Bye 'bye, pooch. I'll pick up
some broccoli.

PONY: Do you...want me to go into my fit
then?

CAPE: (kisses her hard) Yes. And remember,
          Queenie is on your side! (starts drumming)

PONY: (whistles dog whistle to Queenie) If
          she hears anything she'll hear that.
          Okay.

                    (PONY bends three times; her
                    breathing becomes faster, she
                    squeezes her eyes shut, and says
                    "mmmmmmmmmmmmmmm")

CAPE: Choke choke choke choke choke choke choke.

PONY: (has a coughing fit) I got some cake
          stuck.

CAPE: (pats her hard on back) It's only
          wishing Pony -- wishing very very hard.
          Haven't you ever...wished...hard...before?

PONY: It's not just the wishing Cape.

CAPE: Wouldn't you do anything at all to save
          your father's life? Eh? (shakes her)
          Imagine your father, rotting to death,
          DECAYING and--

PONY: (screams) YESS! Yes, yes I would! I
          would do anything, anything, to -- to to
          just have him spit, to have him spit on
          his hanky and clean off my face, have him
          spit and wipe and I could smell it so
          strongly and...

                    (PONY faints and CAPE hugs her,
                    hard. She is dreaming that her
                    dad is wiping his spit all over
                    her face)

PONY: Ha ha ha Dad! Daddy the spit's on my
         face, it's on my... (wakes) Oh. I
         guess I fainted.

CAPE: Are you...all right? (guilty, concerned)
         Are you--

PONY: No. No I'm not okay I don't think I'm
         okay in the least I think I blew a fuse,
         you know? I blew a fuse on account of
         I'm scared! I'm scared 'cause the old me
         is getting killed off by the new me, that
         hatched after we-- This new me -- I'm
         scared -- I'm scared that when I say I'd
         do anything for you that maybe I mean --
         maybe I'd even -- cut my mum and dad!
         (crying) My mum and -- my -- see --
         I've never felt two thoughts at once
         before.

CAPE: (holds her tight) Pony. Why don't you
         go back to Kirkland Lake?

PONY: Do-do-do -- you want me to?

CAPE: No.

PONY: No. So I'm gonna help ya do what ya
         hafta do, 'cause you're right, I love
         you. I love you and-- (takes his hand)
         Is this okay? I marry you...

CAPE: There's Dad coming back in. Why don't
         you go for a walk, eh? (kisses her)
         Everything should be all over by tonight
         ...and then we can go to Cape Race···
         Eh?

                        (PONY, very moved, smiles. She
                        exits. GLIDDEN comes in through
                        the front door)

GLIDDEN: I just had the most disturbing dream -- I
           was standing by the tiger lilies, checking
           for ants, and suddenly a white dingo
           narrowed her eyes and said "Lomia --
           loves you, Glid, she loves you." I
           haven't felt such relief since our
           Airedale Tommy came back after being lost
           for three months. Why did you do that?

CAPE: What?

GLIDDEN: You know bloody well what.

CAPE: She -- she told me that Daddy, honest,
           she did. She said she was gonna leave
           him and stay with you, she--

                    (GLIDDEN hits CAPE across the
                     face. Peat moss tumbles out)

GLIDDEN: Why are you lying? (falls backwards)

CAPE: (crying; cleaning it) I wasn't lying she
           -- she must have -- gone crazy -- I --
           you know how she is, just -- maybe all
           the pressure, or -- I'm sure by tonight
           she will have calmed down, you know what
           she's like when she gets out of bed --
           tonight -- I swear. I swear.

GLIDDEN: But you're having a nervous breakdown!
           You're a twenty-five-year-old man who had
           to move home 'cause he couldn't hack it!
           Why should I believe you?

CAPE: 'Cause it's the only thing keeping you
           alive, Dad.

GLIDDEN: You know NOTHING about what is keeping
          me alive. Nothing. (starts to go; stops)
          I would be grateful if you would keep
          your hands off your drums whilst I attempt
          to have a rest. Thank you... 'Member
          what I always told you? 'Member? In
          the game <u>tomorrow</u>, DON'T HANG BACK, GET
          IN THERE AND PLAY, don't THINK, just get
          in the bloody game and PLAY!! You never
          got it, did you? (exits)

CAPE: No I didn't.

                    (CAPE hears PASCAL approaching,
                    whistling self-consciously.
                    CAPE gets the three hard balls.
                    PASCAL is drawn back to CAPE.
                    CAPE goes to meet him and
                    throws a fast one at PASCAL,
                    who, surprised, catches it.
                    PONY watches this scene from
                    the watching place)

PASCAL: Owww. That's like a belly flop but --
          with the hands...<u>stings</u>--

CAPE: Give it here. Throw it.

PASCAL: I -- I can't. I can't throw, I'm terrible
          at it. Really you should have seen me
          in baseball games. I can't throw --
          hand-eye coordination I guess.

                    (PASCAL puts the ball on the
                    floor. CAPE picks it up)

CAPE: Why don't you try?

                    (CAPE throws. PASCAL catches.
                    CAPE taunts him)

          Daddy's little girl!

                    (PASCAL hesitates)

          Come onnn-- Come on!

                    (PASCAL throws. CAPE throws the
                    ball back, hard and quick.
                    PASCAL misses it, but picks it
                    up and strokes it nervously)

CAPE: You're back early. Where's Mum?

PASCAL: Oh I left her -- looking at apartments...
             I -- I hate that kind of shit, you know?

                    (CAPE is giving him no response)

             It's dull -- looking for apartments,
             shopping-- It makes me so -- tired--

CAPE: Is that why you came back?... (long
             pause) Hey. Try to hit me in the head.

PASCAL: Why?

CAPE: TRY TO HIT ME IN THE HEAD.

PASCAL: (rolls ball along floor) If you -- do a
             headstand it'll -- get you right in the
             cortex.

                    (CAPE, looking at PASCAL, picks
                    up the ball and throws it full
                    force at PASCAL. He does the
                    same with the others. PASCAL
                    falls. CAPE gets him down.
                    PASCAL, fighting tears,
                    surrenders)

             What's the matter, eh?

PASCAL: (whispers) Why do you keep looking at me
             with that--

CAPE: Why... Because-- I -- <u>know</u> you.
           (lies on top of PASCAL) Yeah...I know
           you SO well, the way you looked -- what
           you thought -- you thought about me...
           I know you, and I KNOW that you love me.
           (long kiss)

PASCAL: Oh. (pushes up) Oh GOD -- Mother --
           fu -- Cape. Cape -- I-I have to make a
           confession -- I-I have to tell you what
           I've done...

CAPE: I know what you've done.

                    (CAPE is close behind PASCAL)

PASCAL: Please, please understand, and don't hate
           me. Oh GOD don't hate me your -- well
           -- just like -- doing that -- after
           doing that with <u>her</u>, your mother, I felt
           so -- sick, I couldn't help it I -- I
           went to the Rainbow, you know? And I
           don't know why, but I showed them, I
           showed them all how she sucks, how she
           sucks and sucks her teeth and juts out
           her jaw when she... It's not my fault,
           it was my mouth, my mouth, it yakked
           and yakked and wouldn't stop yakking and
           they all laughed so I told them again,
           I showed them, I showed them the face
           till they could all make it -- now each
           time any one says "Lo," or even "woman,"
           everybody in the room sucks their teeth
           and juts out their jaws -- even right
           behind her back, like -- like yesterday
           at the crosslights-- (pause) Why?
           Tell me, tell me why did I do that?
           Why am I so bad, why?

CAPE: You're not bad, you're wonderful. And
            I know why you did that. I know you...
            (strokes his face) You're wonderful...
            And you need to be taken care of. (picks
            him up) Now. Go to my room, take off
            your clothes, and lie on your stomach.

                        (They go into CAPE's room. PONY
                        has been watching and listening.
                        She softly sings, "You're my
                        dog, my doggie dog." She is
                        just barely hanging together,
                        feels badness coming on, does
                        "see no evil" with hands over
                        eyes, trying to fight badness)

PONY: No. I'm not turning bad. I can't be, I
            can't be, 'member? I'm the girl that won
            the Miss Graciousness award -- at Camp
            Bearmack -- in 1963. (gasp) The Miss
            Graciousness award. I won it. I won it.
            (whistles) Queenie -- Queenie, oh
            Queenie I miss you, 'cause (sings)
            You're my doooog, my doggie dogg, I
            loved ya soooo I always will -- and your
            eyes do shine so bright and clear my
            Queenie dear my dear -- my--

                        (PONY starts to breathe heavily,
                        quickly. She feels a deep,
                        painful hunger, and hears or
                        senses Queenie. She is breaking
                        apart. Blackout. Drums sound.
                        Lights come up on PASCAL
                        standing in the outside area.
                        He takes a ball out of his pocket.
                        Like a cat, he rolls it then
                        falls on it, rolls it... CAPE
                        hides where PONY was earlier
                        in order to watch. We hear the

                click-clack of LOMIA's heels.
                PASCAL is alert, nervous.
                LOMIA runs to PASCAL and hugs
                him)

LOMIA: Oh foof I missed you so much!! You were
mean not to come with me I -- I -- I saw
a blind man on the bus and the thought
of being blind made me feel so dizzy
that I had to lie down on the floor of
the bus! I was sure I was going to
faint! But -- I suppose it was good to
make me go myself because I didn't --
faint -- and -- oh. Everything is
burned, or smoked, at least -- and -- and
there are two apartments we have to look
at tomorrow.

                (PASCAL is playing with the
                ball)

What are you doing? (kisses his neck)
I'm not in a hurry to go back in there
either. Noooo-- (changes) Pascy.
Pascy I can hear my food digesting.
I can hear it! I can hear it being
broken by the enzymes and floating
along in my bloodstream like cows in
a flood in India -- oh it's dreadful,
Pascal, say something to make it go
away -- my hands are cold as death
of course...Paascy--

PASCAL: You what? You can...hear your food?
You know I can't relate to that
schizo-shit -- just...just...I --
wish...that you would just...shut up!

                    (PASCAL walks away gritting his
                    teeth. He speaks under his
                    breath)

PASCAL: Shutup shutupshutupshutupshuchchch...

LOMIA: What's wrong, foofy, what's happened?
            (pause)

PASCAL: Nothing. Nothing has happened.
            (not looking at her)

LOMIA: Look at me, Pascal. Pascal. Pascal, why
            won't you look at me? LOOK AT ME!! Oh
            Lord oh my God when I can't look at
            somebody it's because they repulse me
            because I...HATE them is...is that what
            you...feel about me now? Is that what...

PASCAL: ...I don't...hate you.

LOMIA: Then what...is it...to -- do I have
            spittle on the corner of my mouth is is
            -- my neck starting to bag -- what --
            please just tell me it's okay...

PASCAL: No. It's -- not -- it's -- not okay.

LOMIA: You DO hate me.

PASCAL: Of course I don't, I--

LOMIA: Ohh (this let-down is familiar) but you
            don't...want...me any more?! Wh-why? Why,
            Pascal, what have I done? I haven't
            gained weight. Or grown hair on my
            belly--

PASCAL: STOP. It's not...YOU, Lomia, it's me.
            Gord, Gordon; from OAKVILLE; something's
            -- snapped -- I fainted on the way home,

PASCAL: (cont'd)
I -- just blacked out and fell on the
sidewalk and when I woke up, a...spell
was broke. I'm different I'm Gord, Gord
I got...different blood now I'm not I'm
not who I -- who -- who -- you--

LOMIA: Poor baby what are you talking about?

PASCAL: PLEASE? (goes down to floor)

LOMIA: (gently) What are you talking about?

PASCAL: (biting his hand) Please...just...leave
me alone.

LOMIA: But...how could all this have happened
so...suddenly just yesterday you said I
was your...look (very close, caressing)
just...turn the clock back! Turn the
clock back, yes, here, look it's last
night, remember? It's last night and
I'm -- I'm lying on your stomach counting
your breaths, you don't mind, you don't
mind at all! You--

                (PASCAL violently throws LOMIA
                off with a sound like a rabid
                bear. She attacks him)

PIG! VILE, POISONOUS PISS FAGGOT PIG I
WILL RIP YOUR BLOODY...

                (LOMIA goes for PASCAL's throat.
                PASCAL stops her hands, holds
                her)

PASCAL: You love it Mrs. Race. (violent, but
terrified like a small boy) You LOVE it
and you know it you think it's SEXY.

LOMIA: Take a spoon and pop out my eyeballs, shave off my nipples, you (high-pitched, crouching, incredulous) sooooooo cruuuuuuuuuellllll!!

PASCAL: YOU MADE ME CRUEL... "Squeeze me harder limpprick, pretend you hate me that I'm a dirty slut" you you ALWAYS said that and "Tell me, tell me I'm a fat putrid sow but you'll fuck me anyways," you you you made me cruel (crying) I -- I -- I still went to church when I first met you, I still took the communion host--

LOMIA: DON'T...take those...things...out of bed -- you know I was -- playing I was just--

PASCAL: You wanted to be treated like shit. YOU WANTED TO BE TREATED LIKE SHIT!

LOMIA: ...only because when you treated me like ...fecal matter, the pins and needles would start, see? See? I could begin to...I have never... (looks at him; sighs) you. You don't...understand me.

PASCAL: No. No, and I don't...want to... Sorry... Sorry. You were just a..."neat idea," I guess... Yeah. A neat... something to make me...? HAPPEN-to-glow ...I don't know you, and you don't know me...and...I don't know me...ALL I know, is that I want to go home. I want to go home...find...the Easy Tree I could climb it. I had no trouble climbing it...I want to find the Easy Tree and sit in it. Just...sit in it, okay? (turns to go)

LOMIA: (quietly) Aren't you going to give me
           a...KICK...before you go?

PASCAL: You -- really are...enjoying this, aren't
           you? You're just...bathing in it...
           you're LOVING...being...TRASHED!!
           (begins to leave)

LOMIA: PASCALLLL...

PASCAL: There is nothing...I can do for you.

LOMIA: Yes there is. Yes there is, foofy. You
           can...feed me. You can stuff me! You
           can stuff me and stuff me and stuff me
           till my skin won't hold any more fat and
           it bursts. And then, then you can burn
           me!

PASCAL: You're sick.

LOMIA: For wanting to be fed?

PASCAL: See you around.

LOMIA: Where?

PASCAL: Somewhere.

LOMIA: Watch out limpdick, I'm a duststorm!!
           I am a duststorm and I'm going to tear
           out your face and eyes and (pause; to
           herself) I'm not a duststorm, I'm a
           carrot. A carrot with its head chopped
           off. CHOPPED OFF. I can't...hear them,
           I can't see them and I like it-- But
           ...I'm choking. I'm choking and I don't
           know what to do! What...do you do when
           you don't know what to do? You...go
           home? Do you go home? Yes, you go

LOMIA: (cont'd)
where you have to be-cause...the sun
has gone down and our mothers are
calling so...no more Kick the Can, I
have to be...home... Home, yes, even
though it's too warm to sleep, with
my...husband, my husband, and my son.
Yes. I'll stay here where I'm supposed
to be, and I won't leave again. Here.
And it'll all...be okay, won't it?...
Won't it?

(LOMIA goes into bedroom to have
a rest. A percussive sound
should cover the blackout.
Lights come up on CAPE and
GLIDDEN)

GLIDDEN: I...used to be able to eat half a dozen
eggs and a pound of bacon at a sitting.

CAPE: And you will again.

GLIDDEN: I'm afraid...not.

CAPE: I was telling you the truth, Dad. She
wants to be your wife again. Any minute
now, she is going to walk through that--

(Sound of skateboard is heard)

GLIDDEN: Oh. Oh there's that lovely...sound again.

CAPE: (yelling, teasing) THAT MAID IS SURE
TAKING HER TIME WITH OUR TEAAAA!

GLIDDEN: Don't -- don't tease her she's a nice
little girl... She...reminds me of
Gravenhurst.

(PONY enters with tea tray)

PONY: I didn't take that much time.

CAPE: Awwwwwww.

GLIDDEN: (winks) Don't let him get to you...

CAPE: Look at the way she blushes, in blotches!

PONY: Look, um, I don't like to be teased,
            okay? At all. I just don't appreciate
            it, okay? (pouring tea)

GLIDDEN: (tastes it) Oh. Did you...heat the pot
            first dearie?

PONY: There's nothing the matter with the tea,
            the tea is fine.

CAPE: Hey sweet, why don't you just get him
            another cup.

GLIDDEN: Oh no no no, a piece of toast will be
            fine...

PONY: Okay, okay, there's something the matter
            with the tea, I poisoned it, okay? Here
            if there's something the matter with it,
            I'll get you a new one, okay?

GLIDDEN: Please, don't bother, just sit down and--

PONY: JUST GIVE IT TO ME... Oh forget it,
            just forget it, I don't need this
            any more--

CAPE: PONY...

PONY: YOU just -- leave me alone!! Leave
            me alone, okay? (exits)

GLIDDEN: She's not a pothead, is she?

CAPE: No. No.

GLIDDEN: She better not be.

CAPE: (gets up) I think she's just -- PONY?
           PONY?

PONY: WHAT?

CAPE: What are you doing?

PONY: I'm EATING.

CAPE: WHAT?

PONY: I SAID I'M EATING. Can't ya see I'm
           starving? (comes out with batter all
           over her face) I'm starving to death,
           okay? I NEED TO--

CAPE: Pony. Pony why don't you just put on the
           brakes, and go wash your--

PONY: NO!! NO I WILL NOT WASH MY FACE I AM
           VERY BUSY EATING!

GLIDDEN: Have -- have you tried Weight Watchers,
           dear, my wife had a great success with
           them, they--

PONY: Weight Watchers? Weight Watchers? Will
           Weight Watchers give me back my Pony,
           my--

GLIDDEN: Look, dearie, my wife used to be an eater
           too -- you'll pull through. Just thank
           bloody Christ you're not in wartime in a
           self-dug ditch about to be shot through
           the temples.

PONY: Sir, I would give my eye-teeth to be in
            the war. At least I would know what the
            hell I was supposed to do.

CAPE: Pony, one little pig-out is nothing!

PONY: Look, it's a lot worse than you know,
            Cape, a lot worse; if you knew the truth
            you would hate my blankety-blank guts.

GLIDDEN: Dear oh dear that's rather strong
            language, isn't it?

CAPE: We wouldn't Pony--

PONY: You would HATE MY GUTS you stupid fool!
            I didn't mean that I like you I love
            you but I'm not, I'm not a nice girl
            like you think, see, I'm a pig girl,
            a slut slutty slut pig, see? (snorts
            three times) See? I -- you know what I
            did today? You're not gonna believe
            this but you better 'cause it's true,
            it's me it's P-I-G me -- I didn't go for
            a walk like you said, I listened and I
            watched you and it freaked it freaked
            me right out till I was soo soo hungry
            I just -- I just didn't know what to do
            -- ever been that hungry? Math class used
            to make me hungry, eh, but not like this,
            this was E-merg time so so -- no listen,
            listen and don't interrupt. I went to
            your kitchen -- and I go through the
            cupboards one by one and I see the flour!
            The Monarch flour so I take it out, see,
            I take it out and I mix it with water, a
            whole bunch, and I eat it and eat it and
            eat it till it's coming up my throat
            but it's not enough! It wasn't enough,
            you know that feeling? I needed

PONY:

(cont'd)
something else, something to make it
perfect, but I didn't know what,
I needed help sooo bad like the time I
was lost in the snow in -- the dark and
woulda froze to death if it wasn't for
my best helper of all ever my Queenie
my dog! My white dead dog that I loved
more than anything. She'd save me now
even though she was dead. She saved me
then and I knew I knew so -- I listened
and she told me, she told me what to do
and I did it, I did it, yeah, I crept
down the stairs like a burglar, down to
the cellar and over to the freezer and
I opened it whew! Cold air! And I
took out my Swiss Army knife and I
slashed the bags open and -- there they
were! The dachshunds! Erica, Gretchen,
and Hans, her dogs just lying there
dead and I did it I did it I sliced --
off chunks of their fro-frozen flesh --
and I stuffed 'em here, in the sides of
my mouth like a squirrel -- yeah, so
so I run up the stairs as fast as I can
and I get out the cake mix, Dominion
brown fudge and I mix in the dogflesh
and I put it in my hand I eat it and I
eat it and I eat it till I almost faint,
till it's coming out my tear ducts but
I don't care! I don't care, eh, 'cause
I feel good, I feel clean and then you
come down and -- the sight of you makes
me bring up! I bring it all up and it
stinks and it's coming and I can't stop
it and then the toilet clogs, but it's
still coming up, it's burning my throat
so what do I do? I gotta put it
somewhere, so I -- I -- throw it up

PONY: (cont'd)
in the -- I'm sorry, I really am and
forgive me please but if you want to know
where I threw up your dogs, smell your
smell, smell -- smell, smell your cups,
suckers!! Smell your cups!! SEE? I told
you you would hate me, but I couldn't
help it, I... (pause) Wanna hear a joke?
Fat people practise girth control!! Oh
ho ho ho that was a good one, eh? That
was cute, I am a funny bunny, eh? Eh you
guys? Oh. Oh please don't look like that
I -- I think I'm okay now, honest -- I
freaked out 'cause of all that stuff
that's been goin' on I -- really was just
joking, don't look so SERIOUS!! I really
was sort of kidding I-- I don't know
what.

> (PONY freezes for a beat, then
> exits. CAPE smells his cup,
> puts it down)

CAPE: I buried the dachshunds last week, Dad.
Dad?

GLIDDEN: (feels very dizzy) What is high blood
pressure, son? What IS it?

CAPE: I don't know, Dad, too much blood?

GLIDDEN: This young...woman...is she...in love
with you, Cape?

CAPE: I...think...so...

GLIDDEN: You could do with what she's got...

CAPE: I guess.

GLIDDEN: ...I remember when you couldn't
           stay up on the rope tow, kept...
           bell-belly flopping over in the snow
           -- up your wrists, down your shirt,
           holding everybody up... "Daaaad,
           daaaad"...

PONY: I heard every word you fuckers said.

GLIDDEN: Good heavens.

CAPE: Pony.

PONY: Oh DON'T say that you know what I mean,
           for crikey's sake just gimme a break,
           gimme a break, okay? I miss my dog. I
           miss my Queenie and my mice just...

CAPE: (embraces PONY) We're not mad at you
           Pony.

PONY: But... (sobbing) I like, get the
           impression that you think what I did was
           serious! Like...out of control.

GLIDDEN: We all lose the wheel sometime--

PONY: Oh no! No, I was just joking, I really
           was. Wow? Did I fool you?

CAPE: Pony, please.

GLIDDEN: Are you on one of those rock concert
           pills?

PONY: Boy, that's amazing, 'cause like -- I
           didn't think you guys were that gullible
           -- like that was just a comedy show I was
           planning for shopping centres, like for
           my job! It's just a show!

CAPE: Pony!

PONY: Don't be mad.

GLIDDEN: We're not "mad," Pony dear, we're...

CAPE: We're <u>friends</u>.

PONY: But I'm not just your friend. <u>Oh no</u>
          that's what I was <u>afraid</u> you were
          thinking. I'm--

                    (LOMIA enters. GLIDDEN hides
                    any trace of moss)

GLIDDEN: Lom!! I didn't realize you'd got back
          from your -- jaunt. How-- How's the
          apartment? Is it a total loss or--

LOMIA: Well, almost. Everything's, you know,
          covered in smoke -- I just -- when I got
          back I thought I'd lie down for fifteen
          minutes and suddenly it's dinner time!
          Hello, Pony, how nice that you stayed...

CAPE: Um, if you'll excuse us, Pony and I
          have some -- business... Pony?

                    (CAPE and PONY leave. They go
                    outside to the watching place)

GLIDDEN: You -- you must be starved. Can I get
          you something, throw a slice of ham
          between a couple pieces of toast. Or
          some po-po-potato salad? Or--

LOMIA: No, no I -- oh. I guess I will have a
          slice of toast. Just. One. Thank you.

GLIDDEN: Just one... (rushes to kitchen to put
          toast in, rushes back)

LOMIA: Thanks again for that lovely...lunch!

GLIDDEN: Yes well, I'm afraid it was...marred
            by my gullibility...

LOMIA: Oh oh please that was...

GLIDDEN: You must be in a hurry to get out of
            here.

LOMIA: No.

GLIDDEN: No?

LOMIA: Glidden I have to...tell...ask...you
            something.

GLIDDEN: You want more cash? Sure thing
            right a--

LOMIA: NO! No no no it's not that it's...
            I... I'm too shy to· say it.

GLIDDEN: Too shy? Is it medi-physi-medical?

LOMIA: No.

GLIDDEN: Well...if it embarrasses you don't...

LOMIA: But I have to...I -- look I just
            wanted to ask you if I could-- I
            can't. I just can't.

GLIDDEN: Look. Pretend if you DON'T, then a
            million people will die.

LOMIA: Okay.

GLIDDEN: Go on.

LOMIA: A million... Glid I want to stay here.
            If you'll...have...me.

                    (GLIDDEN awkwardly kisses LOMIA,
                    a long kiss. She tries as hard
                    as she can to be passionate.
                    He speaks, in a whisper, out of
                    breath. They are face to face)

GLIDDEN: ...if you really -- want me...a...sort
            of...party hat of a man...

LOMIA: You are not you are not a party hat of
            a man.

PONY: Wow! That's it! That's it, eh, I guess
            we did it! Eh?

CAPE: Yeah...yeah, I guess -- we did...

PONY: Crikes he looks glad...hey, how come so
            glum?... Oh, I know. I know, it's
            'cause of what we did to get this...to
            Pascal and that, eh?

CAPE: What I did, what I did, Pony, not what
            you did.

PONY: I might as well o' done it 'cause I wished
            it on...I stood up there and I watched
            you and I wished it on -- for us.

                    (During PONY's speech, GLIDDEN
                    goes to the kitchen)

CAPE: Pony, you don't understand; I did it all
            for myself -- I never thought of you
            once.

PONY: That's not my opinion.

CAPE: Why? Why don't you see--

PONY: My opinion is that you are forgiven by the Holy Ghost.

CAPE: Why?

PONY: Sorry sinners get GRACE, that's what Brother Farney said. Because you're sorry. IT'S ME THAT WON'T BE FORGIVEN, 'CAUSE I'm not sorry. Not at all. So -- do you feel the change yet?

CAPE: What change?

PONY: The change you said'd come in you if ya saved your dad... Has it -- started?

CAPE: No.

PONY: It'll come, it will! Why would Queenie have lied -- it'll come when it'll come when we head off for our holidays.

CAPE: Holidays?

PONY: Poor guy you must be bushed! To Cape Race! What we been talkin' about the whole time!

CAPE: No. No, no don't you see?

PONY: (shocked, shaking all over) Boy, does my hair feel tangly.

> (PONY leaves to fetch brush. GLIDDEN enters carrying toast on a fork. He holds it up then gives it to LOMIA. She holds it up for the duration of the scene)

GLIDDEN: I -- guess Cape has told you about my -- darn--

LOMIA: I think we can beat it, don't you?

GLIDDEN: I hope so... (touches her; they look
           at each other)

LOMIA: I am...so -- so, so -- sorry for having
           ...I <u>really</u> am sorry!? (can't believe it
           herself) Me! I -- <u>am</u>.

GLIDDEN: I know you are...

LOMIA:·   I don't deserve...your...forgiveness.

GLIDDEN: (covers her mouth with his hand)
           Shhhhhhh... (strokes her hair) I'm
           the one that...almost...lost faith...

                    (PONY returns to where CAPE is,
                     brush in hand)

PONY: This -- this isn't 'cause of that routine
           I tried out on you guys--

CAPE: No.

PONY: Then...why?

CAPE: Because I'm not -- like other men...

PONY: Oh yes you are, you need what other men
           need.

CAPE: I do?

PONY: I think the word you used was ecstasy.

CAPE: Yes.

PONY: What do you expect me to do?

CAPE: Go back to your fix-it stand. I'm sure there are plenty...

    (PONY throws the brush on the floor)

    Pony, if I could love anybody, I would love you. But it's not going to happen.

PONY: But you said.

CAPE: I know I said, I thought it would. But it hasn't. And it won't. The white dog never existed.

PONY: Oh yes she did. She did so exist! You're just bummed out 'cause of shame 'cause you know we did wrong, but ya shouldn't 'cause we're in it together, you and me, we're bad guys--

CAPE: NO. We're not in it together. Just go home, please? Go home to your family and you'll be okay, you'll--

PONY: How could I go home, eh? How could I go home to the very people I would have Judas-licked for you? They wouldn't know me anyways 'cause the old Pony's almost squished but -- but it was worth it to me for you, anything was, ANYTHING was worth havin' YOU and now I don't, I don't have you and oh my Gol -- oh my Gol -- oh my--

CAPE: YOU NEED TO GET AWAY FROM ME, JUST--

PONY: NO!! No, don't you understand! I got a mission, I got a mission to fulfill, to help you save you and I'm gonna! I'm Crikey well gonna save you and...

(PONY crouches down, goes into
her concentration. She turns
in the crouch, around and
around)

PONY: I'VE GOT IT! I got it! Holy OH my feet
are buzzing--

CAPE: What?

PONY: You watch, you watch, my darling, I'm
gonna swoop down inside myself and pull
out the old Pony, and I'm gonna give her
over to you. And when she's inside you,
you're gonna be saved.

CAPE: Shhhhhhh.

(CAPE feels PONY's forehead.
When he touches her, she wraps
her arms around him)

You feel so hot... Why do you want me
so much?

PONY: 'Cause. You're the only husband I ever
had.

(CAPE hugs PONY very hard. PONY
enters the house)

LOMIA: When he first -- told me he was leaving I
-- felt -- like a carrot! Headless --
cold -- I thought I'd lost my power to
hold -- to -- you know, enchant! I
haven't, have I? I'm -- I mean I'm not
just another middle-aged woman--

GLIDDEN: You're a goddess, darl, a sphinx, and
the best darn hostess-- Hold on a
minute, hold on, are you saying that
he -- left you?

LOMIA: He brought it up--

GLIDDEN: If he hadn't -- brought it up, then you
would still be -- with him? (clutching
his stomach)

LOMIA: Oh Glidden, that's not fair, it's--

GLIDDEN: Just tell me the truth, please.

LOMIA: I wasn't myself when I was with him. I
was counterfeit, so it doesn't count.

GLIDDEN: Listen to me, Lomia. I am your husband
and I know you. Do you understand that?
I know about your...

LOMIA: You do?

GLIDDEN: And I love you. Still. Okay? (starts
to go upstairs) Okay.

LOMIA: Where are you going?

GLIDDEN: Just to get -- something -- don't -- go
away.

LOMIA: I won't -- I can't -- are you--?

GLIDDEN: I'm okay. I'm okay, darl, and you'll be
okay if you let me in. Will you let me
in?

LOMIA: (nods) I'll try.

                (GLIDDEN goes into the bedroom,
                his body crumpling. He pours
                peat moss over his head)

LOMIA: "Let me in, let me in, let in IN" WHAT
          DOES HE MEAN? I know what he means, but
          I CAN'T, I'm SHUT, I'm JAMMED I -- ohh
          GOD let me let him--

                (GLIDDEN comes out to the
                landing with the large bag
                of peat moss. He falls on
                it, hugging it to his body)

GLIDDEN: Darl? Darl? I'm sorry I can't hold it
          off any longer I can't stop it any--

                (GLIDDEN collapses onto the bag,
                breathing with great difficulty.
                He is in a coma)

LOMIA: Dooon't make that death face poochie
          take it off take it -- please, please
          stop that breathing stop that -- Gliddie!
          Gliddie remember when we were first
          married you would lie in bed and sing,
          while I danced to your song? We did that
          almost every night, remember? Well let
          me make you better with that dance,
          watch me, watch me closely and sing the
          song, you remember it... (starts up the
          stairs doing a violent, erotic strip
          tease) I'm the LAAAAADEEEE who LADDDIES
          ...LOVE to adore, the WOMAN (dancing
          up steps to GLIDDEN) who WOM-BATS DIE
          longing FOR -- CREATED from TIGERS...
          and GOOSEFEATHER DOWN I'm the LADY,
          BOM BOM DE BOM, the jewel of the town...

          (LOMIA bends over, rips her
          nylons from ankle to crotch,
          and looks at GLIDDEN)

LOMIA: It hasn't worked. Oh no oh help me
          Glidden--?

          (Sound of skateboard is heard.
          GLIDDEN giggles, sits up and
          says with irony)

GLIDDEN: Oh no, not YOU!! (looks at audience)
          HELP YOURSELVES TO TOAST, EVERYBODY!!

          (GLIDDEN dies. LOMIA looks,
          screams a forced scream, then
          stops, knowing this is
          fraudulent)

LOMIA: It's no use.

          (Outside, CAPE gets a flash
          of danger. He runs around
          to the back of the house)

Oh Glidden, FOR-give me For-- (her hand
on her stomach, she feels some fat)
Faaaa-t-- (feels a totally unfamiliar
feeling; something inside her is
cracking) Oh Gliddie I think...I
THINK...

          (LOMIA takes two deep breaths.
          LOMIA's face must be very
          close to GLIDDEN's; her body
          must look as if a strange
          chemical has entered it. CAPE
          enters carrying PONY who has
          hanged herself. The rope
          dangles. CAPE sinks down,
          stunned. He looks up and sees
          that GLIDDEN is dead)

(PONY rises, walks to edge of
stage, and directs the following
speech to where the projectionist
would be if the theatre were a
cinema)

PONY: Excuse me, could you call the projectionist,
please? He's my Dad -- I just have to
talk to him for a second -- I know -- but
the thing can run on its own, we both
know that -- besides, this is an emergency!
Yeah! Thanks, thanks a lot... (peering)
Dad? I can see the dustbeam but I can't
see you oh there you are hi! Hi... It's
me -- no, no I'm not back, I'm not even
in the Kirk, actually, I'm just -- like
this is gonna totally weird you out, but
-- I had to appear to you like this 'cause
-- in a couple of hours you're gonna hear
that -- don't freak out -- that I passed
myself on and -- like -- I didn't want
you to get too down about it so I thought
I'd come and tell you myself that -- it's
not at all a bad thing. It's quite nice
if you just give in to it. You know the
feeling when you're falling asleep and ya
jump awake 'cause you dreamt you slipped
on a stair? Well it's like if you stayed
in the slip -- if you dove right down into
it and held your breath till you came out
the other end. I'm in the holding your
breath part right now, so I'm not sure
what's on the other end, but I feel like
I'm so big I'd barely fit into Kirk
Community Centre -- it's weird, but...Dad?
Dad? The main reason I came was to let
you know that I didn't...kill myself
'cause I couldn't hack it or because

PONY: (cont'd)
the man I loved couldn't love me back,
it was 'cause...I was invaded, Dad, Dad,
<u>filled</u> by the worst evil...you ever
imagined -- I guess it happened when
I fell in love, on account of I had to
open my mouth so wide to let the love in
that the evil came in, too...and living
with it was just like being skinned alive;
worse pain even than your kidney stones,
and <u>we</u> know how bad <u>they</u> were. Now the
pain has stopped, and there's still the
old Pony to give to my husband: 'cause
he needs it, Dad, like a blood
transfusion <u>he</u> needs it, and just like
Mum would give you anything you needed,
I'm gonna give myself to him. No, we
didn't get papers, but he's my husband
all right. His name is Cape Race, like
the place, eh? Oh yeah, I told him
about your mice and he was really
impressed and uh -- tell Wade there's a
stereo store down here that's looking
for someone and Mum -- tell Mum not to
go into the ditch about this 'cause I
know they're gonna let me come visit --
to...straighten her fingers and...give
her alcohol rubs... Well...I have to --
finish my dive now... Oh Dad I'm so big
now I'd never fit back on earth. Love...
Pony.

(CAPE, at first in shock, but
then thinking that she must be
alive, slowly walks up to her,
to take her in his arms. She
says her last word, "Pony," into
his chest. He holds her, then
turns and turns with her, making
a very high-pitched, mounting

> sound that breaks into a primal
> scream. He cries, lies with
> her on the floor)

CAPE: You didn't have to -- <u>why</u> for...me??
For <u>me</u>?

LOMIA: (in shock, but cognizant of what has
happened) Because they...loved...us, I
guess.

CAPE: We're not...WORTH...

LOMIA: No!

> (LOMIA looks at CAPE. They both
> feel, hope, that a change is
> taking place; deep within them
> something has cracked. Maybe
> the only feeling they are
> experiencing is guilt, but that
> is something)

CAPE: Do you think it will make...any...
difference?

> LOMIA looks up. Her hope
> shows in her eyes. CAPE just
> does not know.

> Blackout.

> The End